BLOOD COVENANT

BLOOD COVENANT

✦

GOD'S CHOSEN RELATIONSHIP

A. Geoffrey Carr, Ph.D

iUniverse, Inc.

New York Lincoln Shanghai

BLOOD COVENANT
GOD'S CHOSEN RELATIONSHIP

iUniverse books may be ordered through booksellers or by contacting:

iUniverse
2021 Pine Lake Road, Suite 100
Lincoln, NE 68512
www.iuniverse.com
1-800-Authors (1-800-288-4677)

ISBN-13: 978-0-595-38866-0 (pbk)
ISBN-13: 978-0-595-83245-3 (ebk)
ISBN-10: 0-595-38866-3 (pbk)
ISBN-10: 0-595-83245-8 (ebk)

Printed in the United States of America

This book is dedicated to all who desire to know the hidden depths of God and be enlightened not only in their mind but also in their spirit.

The book was written in the first instance to meet the need of students in a Christian Education Programme addressing the need for researched material on the subject matter due to the lack of published books on such an important matter which is considered to be fundamental to the Christian Faith.

This book is also dedicated to all those seeking stable roots and foundation in someone greater than themselves, trusting that it may be a source of encouragement and blessing in your quest for knowledge of the deeper things of God

Contents

SECTION 1

CHAPTER 1   THE CONCEPT OF COVENANT 3

CHAPTER 2   TYPES OF COVENANT. 7

CHAPTER 3   HEATHENISTIC CEREMONY DETAILS 10

CHAPTER 4   HEBREW/BIBLICAL CEREMONY
DETAILS 14

CHAPTER 5   THE ULTIMATE BLOOD COVENANT
RELATIONSHIP 26

SECTION 2

CHAPTER 6   SO WHAT? 45

CHAPTER 7   WHO AM I?. 50

CHAPTER 8   WHAT DO I HAVE?. 57

CHAPTER 9   WHERE AM I GOING? 65

CHAPTER 10   CONCLUSION 71

SECTION 1

1

THE CONCEPT OF COVENANT

The subject of this book was a great mystery to me over twenty years ago although at that time I had been a Christian for some thirty years. This experience fairly much sums up the situation in the Christian Church today throughout Western Society and is the basic reason for the great weakness in the standing and understanding of basic Christian teaching and the relationship of understanding to Biblical Truth. I now hold the opinion in the light of the experience of having discovered by God's Grace the wonder and the certainty of my relationship to my God through Blood Covenant that I have an authority and a standing in my God because of the New Blood Covenant that Jesus Christ has brought in through His time of Ministry on the earth and the Father's Plan of Salvation that He now intercedes for us in the Heavenlies.

The problems that may beset the reader can easily be identified and are common to most of the Christian Church of our generation in Western Society. These problems evolve around the interaction between that which is spiritual and that which is natural.

In the natural we struggle with the concept of covenant because our Western Society is not familiar with such a concept, with some very few exceptions, and most of Western Society today struggles to identify what a spiritual concept is unless it is either occultish or demonically influenced or some similar variation since most of modern Western Society has become either non-Christian, post-Christian or anti-Christian and looks upon the Bible as something belonging to a past generation. Fortunately, this is not true in all cases but it must be understood from the outset that those who will gain most from the reading of this book will need to have a thorough understanding of the teachings of the Bible at a mature level as they relate to modern society today.

The concept of covenant is apparently a universal concept and understanding in the cultures of primitive societies, but to the Western mind, which looks upon itself as a sophisticated society, it is either dismissed as irrelevant, or for a past era, or is certainly not recognised in what small remains exist. The Hebrews had a blood covenant ritual that was similar to the other nations around them. All nations practiced blood covenant because man instinctively sought this relationship. So this practice was not unique to the Hebrews."[1] "This rite is still observed in the unchanging East; and there are historic traces of it, from time immemorial, in every quarter of the globe; yet it has been strangely overlooked by biblical critics and biblical commentators generally, in these later centuries."[2] With this in mind, it is not without significance that the main last bastion of covenant remains in a Christian Marriage Ceremony, nor is the demise of marriage in Western Society without significance when covenant is thus dismissed. This does not mean to say that many who enter marriage are not unaware of the solemnity or the seriousness of committing to vows that are taken in a ceremony. In order to understand the commitment level of a marriage ceremony it is first necessary to understand the meaning of covenant and the binding effect on the parties entering into covenant as opposed to some sort of verbal arrangement, civil contractual process, or some religious ceremony.

In order to investigate the relevant content and position of Blood Covenant it is necessary to have some sort of standard as our authoritative reference point for both Christian and non-Christian alike and it is the author's position that the Bible represents such a standard, being divinely inspired, its authors moved upon by the leading of the Holy Spirit and its accuracy, despite much discussion down many years, is of such a high standard that men down many generations have been prepared to give their life blood to maintain production of this amazing book which is in our hands today! The arguments that many wish to enter into regarding viewpoints on various translations and the accuracy of such translation is surpassed by far in the theme of the main message of the Bible in its entirety. In this the Blood Covenant is the key thread that is woven through the various books and accounts from the front of the book to the end of the book and therefore a greater understanding of the concept of Blood Covenant and indeed other Covenants that are described in the Biblical accounts is the key to unlocking the significance of many statements that are made, many actions that are taken and indeed many of the pages of subsequent history to the Biblical account continue

---

1.   *Miracle of the Scarlet Thread*—Richard Booker—p27.
2.   *The Blood Covenant*—H. Clay Trumbull—p. 5.

to hold the values that Blood Covenant enshrines from the days of the Creation Story even into our 21st century.

In overview of the ideas discussed so far, the concept of covenant is that two parties come together either as individuals, or for larger groups such as tribes or nations, their representatives would enact the ceremony on their behalf. The resulting arrangement that the parties have in covenant together is far stronger than any contract, either written or verbal. The symbolism that takes place in the covenant ceremony is such that it is both demanding total and absolute commitment to each other in a total life resource interchange, and this level of commitment is not only for the natural life of the individuals, but so long as one partner remains, there is a commitment of support to those who relate to the deceased on the part of the one who committed to the initial covenant. Such a level of commitment in continuity is a concept that the Western Society mind struggles to either understand or come to terms with. Referring to the Bedween involved with Covenant of Brotherhood, Clay Trumbull records "…The brother (in such a covenant) must guard the (other) brother from treachery, and (must) succor him in peril. So far as may be necessary, the one must provide for the wants of the other: and the survivor has weighty obligations on behalf of the family of the deceased."[3] We see this enacted between David and Mephibosheth in 2 Samuel 21:7: *"But the king spared Mephibosheth the son of Jonathan, the son of Saul, because of the Lord's oath that was between them, between David and Jonathan the son of Saul."*

We will see in the subsequent chapters the methodology of bringing about such a relationship as well as from Biblical accounts which refer to the evidence that supports this covenant concept.

---

3.   Ibid—p. 10.

Questions on Chapter 1

1. What are the roots of the concept of Covenant?

2. Why does Western Society have little or no understanding of the concept of Covenant?

3. Within Western Society what ceremony is the last bastion of maintaining Covenant?

4. Name three versions of this ceremony that are listed in the chapter but operate in modern society.

5. Identify the two basic concepts of which the reader needs understanding in order to appreciate covenant.

6. What significance was given in the chapter to the failing of marriage in Western Society?

7. What is the normal level of commitment operated by those coming into covenant?

8. In the event of the death of one of the parties entering covenant, what is expected of the party remaining to the family of the one who has died?

9. What is the level of resource commitment expected of each other of those coming into covenant? Write notes of what you understand about this as a reference for later.

10. Why do you think covenant is so little understood today?

2

TYPES OF COVENANT

Having looked at the concept of covenant it is now necessary to consider what types of covenant we are likely to come across. For this purpose I have broken them down into two main types. Whilst there is some overlap in the content of these types, there are clear distinctions between the two that are both naturally and spiritually significant and the types of society in which they are likely to be found operating.

The two types are (1) Heathenistic and (2) Hebrew/Biblical. In the first type, those entering covenant were of non-Judaistic tribal or national origin and whose religious worship systems had no connection to the God of the Hebrews. The second type is confined entirely to the activities found in the biblical records of the Hebrew nation and relates solely in concept to the Lord God Almighty or Jehovah or other names by which the God of the Hebrews is identified in the biblical records. It is now intended to observe many of the distinctions and activities that take place in the covenant ceremonies and reflect upon the characteristic of the God or gods that relate to the people entering into these types of covenant.

In the first type we can identify in most cases a six-part ceremony conducted by a priest or "holy man" whereas in the second type a nine-part ceremony can be identified from biblical records. It also is conducted by a priest and before God Almighty.

A final part may be added to both these ceremonies in that the relationship to which the parties enter is that of "friendship" i.e. they would refer to each other as friends.

These ceremonies of both types of blood covenant have three basic components to the covenant. These are (1) the oath, which is used as a binding force to maintain the framework, authority and major spiritual content as a basis of the relationship thus securing unity. It was normal to take the oath and swear the oath by naming your god or one of much higher authority than yourself. In order to understand the significance of this it is also necessary to understand the fuller meaning of swearing an oath, and (2) the promise is the second element of the covenant. In this element terms were agreed before entering into covenant and these terms were rehearsed as part of the covenant ceremony before the parties. You may think this is similar to a contract but the terms of the promise that was being made by both parties included a very significant difference to that of a contract. The terms that were included in this promise element showed a sharp distinction in the types of terms of promise made between heathenistic and Hebrew/Biblical covenants. In the former, the terms that were given would be binding promises linked to a plethora of curses at a very deep spiritual level and with the authority of the god by whom the oath was being taken for their effectiveness. On the other hand, in the Hebrew/Biblical covenant the terms of the promise were quite clear as to what would happen if they were broken and the displeasure of Almighty God would be displayed in particular aspects that were named but also for those who kept the terms of the covenant there was major benefit and blessing to be had to the parties that would remain faithful to the promise.

Plans with the purposes that lay behind these concepts would be included and the goals to be attained through the plans would be specified with or without time limits or targets.

(3) The sacrifice of an innocent animal is the third element of The Blood Covenant. This element of the covenant became the most serious and solemn in the eyes of the participants because in sacrificing an innocent animal life, they were agreeing together that this animal's sacrifice was a picture or living symbol, of the level of commitment each to the other. Since there is obviously no future to he had between the parties should either of them lay down their own life, then a symbol and substitute had to be used i.e. a substitute in that the animal was innocent to the covenant, and symbolic in that each party would identify with the animal in its last moments of life to speak on behalf of the parties, by having its life taken as a symbol of the commitment into which those parties were now entering i.e. unto death of both parties.

In selecting the innocent animal to be used on the occasion of the covenant ceremony, it was normal for a perfect specimen in a good state of health to be chosen, thus giving full representation to the state of health of the parties entering covenant and as an indication to the longevity and healthiness of the arrangement being entered into. Since the Hebrews were forbidden by God to consume blood, especially human blood, it follows that an animal sacrifice overcame this difficulty.

"In the few thousand years preceding the neolithic era, even cave paintings became more efficacious if the pigment used was blood. But it was the relations between men and men—and, later man and god—that flesh and blood were to have their most significant role to play. For one man to absorb the blood of another (living or dead) was equivalent of absorbing part of his essence, his force, his nature?[1]

Questions on Chapter 2

1. Identify two basic types of covenant under discussion.

2. Identify the type of society and people that each of these types of covenant were likely to use.

3. How many parts of a ceremony was each type thought to use?

4. What relationship was identified as a common element that could be added as a conclusion to each ceremony?

5. What office was represented at the conducting of all of these types of ceremony?

6. In the Hebrew/Biblical ceremony what major presence was recognised as a contribution to the ceremony?

7. Name the three basic elements discussed that applied to all types of covenant ceremony.

8. Why was an oath sworn by a higher authority as part of the covenant ceremony?

9. Identify three aspects of the terms entered into with consequences.

10. Whose blood was spilt and life taken as part of the ceremony? Identify three characteristics.

---

1. *Flesh and Blood: A History of the Cannibal Compex*—Reay Tannahill

3

HEATHENISTIC CEREMONY DETAILS

In these covenant ceremonies both heathenistic and Hebrew/Biblical, there is a great emphasis on the symbolism of the actions of the participants. We have identified already that there are some considerable common elements to both these ceremonies which would be expected, as we are considering both natural and spiritual aspects of what is going on; therefore those things that are purely natural symbolism at a physical and soulish level, are likely to be common elements to both ceremonies, whereas that which enters the boundary of spiritual significance or representation is likely to show distinction since it is based on very different spiritual standing, relative to each other

Whilst the three basic elements of oath, promise and sacrifice occur in both heathenistic and Hebrew/Biblical ceremonies, the heathenistic covenant ceremony that takes place in the presence of a priest or holy man, is thought to be something based on the following six elements. Not all elements would necessarily be used at one time.

1. Exchange of Gifts

This symbolic exchange of ownership of some limited gift, symbolises the exchange of ALL of each other's assets. This was taken very seriously, and to refuse was to break covenant; thus there was one common pool of material strength and wealth (here we have the basis of common wealth). This area covered not only material/physical gifts, but also assets of all kinds; therefore, when the nations or tribes came together, there was one large army to fight the common enemies and not two small fighting bands as before.

2. <u>A Cup of Wine</u>

The fruit of the grape, which when squeezed produces wine, has always been a symbol representing the blood of each party coming into covenant. Deuteronomy 32:14 clearly identifies wine as the blood of the grape. *"Curds from the cattle, and milk from the flock, with fat of lambs; and rams of the breed of Bashan, and goats, with the choicest wheat; and you drank wine, the blood of grapes."* In the heathenistic covenant, blood from each party or its representative was added to the cup of wine, stirred by the priest, and drunk by both parties until the cup was dry.

3. <u>Incision on Arm or Wrist</u>

As part of the ceremony, each party or their representative, would make a cut which would draw significant blood on either arm or wrist, and as the blood flowed out of this incision it would be dribbled into the cup described above, identifying the very life blood commitment of each party which then became so entwined, as to be irrevocably untangled by being stirred together. Because of this element of the ceremony, the correct term relative to coming into covenant is that you "cut covenant" as opposed to entering or joining or any other word. As part of the ceremony, the incision that had been made would quite often have charcoal from a burnt stick rubbed into it, so that when it healed over a clear black line could be seen. This was used later on as a means of an indicator to opposing armies when a champion soldier would challenge the opposing army to come forward with a representative and there would be a battle of champions. In order to make the choice, the opposing army would well take into consideration the number of incision marks on the challenging champion, thus indicating the number of tribes or nations with whom he had covenant relationship, and would, therefore, be at his disposal should they wish to take on the whole army or, indeed, from other champions that may be selected to fight a champion's battle.

4. <u>A Cup is Stirred</u>

The contents of the bloody cup are now stirred by the priest and consumed by each party in turn until all is consumed. The symbolism here is that my life is now in you, and your life is in me, since blood was taken to represent the life of each party.

5. <u>Wrists Touched</u>

A variation on this part of the ceremony is that either the wrist or arm that had been cut was put together so that the blood flowed from each party into the other, or alternatively each party licked the wound of the other party, bringing about the same result and reinforcing the blood that had been consumed with the wine in the common cup.

6. <u>Pronouncing of Terms</u>

We have previously commented on the terms which were part of the promise element of the ceremony. So seriously did tribes and nations take this element of covenant, especially where a wider community or tribe is concerned, that those found breaking the terms of such a covenant element would bring fear of reprisal upon the whole nation, that the life of the individual who had broken covenant would be taken by members of his own nation or tribe so as to avoid the consequences of covenant breaking to come upon the whole nation or tribe. With this in mind, we can perhaps now understand more fully why some Biblical accounts bring stories of unfaithfulness being declared to higher authority, and also why God would challenge the Hebrew people through the prophets by accusing them of breaking covenant.

This appears to be the limited list of the element of a heathenistic covenant ceremony, but it is quite likely that there would be variations on the ceremony elements or additions to the basic six. It is interesting to note that in Biblical symbolism the number six speaks of the things of man and also note that the use of blood in this ceremony comes from a human source and the concept of a substitutionary death of an innocent animal is not included. It should also be noted that in the Mosaic Law the drinking or consuming of human blood was strictly forbidden and animal blood was only used as part of a sacrifice to the Living God, Jehovah. It would be looked upon by the Hebrew nation as breaking covenant with the Living God. This is also one of the reasons why the Hebrews were forbidden to intermarry with heathenistic nations as well as becoming involved with foreign gods, as this was seen as mingling the "blood line" between the Hebrew nation with whom Almighty God had entered covenant and other heathenistic and occultish gods.

Speaking of the Scythians, Trumball records, "…having poured out wine into a great earthen drinking bowl, they mingle with it the blood of those cutting covenant, striking the body (or of each person having a part in it) with a small knife, or cutting it slightly with a sword. Thereafter they dip into the bowl, sword, arrows, axe, and javelin. But while they are doing this, they make many invokings (of curse upon breach of this covenant); and afterwards, not only those who make the covenant, but those of their followers who are of the highest rank, drink of (the wine mingled with blood)."[1]

Questions on Chapter 3

1. How many component parts were identified as a minimum to the heathenistic covenant ceremony?

2. What is the significance of this number in terms of numerology?

3. List the individuals who would be present at the ceremony and give the alternatives and the authority under which each individual would operate.

4. Explain the significance of the following in the ceremony:

   a. exchange of gifts

   b. use of a cup of wine

   c. the making of an incision that would cause blood to flow.

5. Having established the above three components, list three further components to the ceremony and explain concisely what happens at each step.

6. Explain the use of human blood in this ceremony and where and why it contrasts with the Hebrew/Biblical ceremony.

7. Explain why within a heathen tribe or nation a covenant breaker may have his life taken once his activity was known.

8. What military use did the permanent mark of the incision have in times of confrontation? What message did it convey?

9. What level of authority did a heathenistic covenant have?

10. What sharp contrast is there in the Promise or Terms section of a heathenistic ceremony and that of a Hebrew/Biblical ceremony?

---

1. *The Blood Covenant*—H. Clay Trumbull—p. 62.

4

HEBREW/BIBLICAL CEREMONY DETAILS

In this chapter we will investigate the Biblical record surrounding parts of the Hebrew/Biblical Ceremony that are recorded. It should be noted that not all of the nine elements discussed occur in one area of Scripture but we can identify these elements in various books of the Old Testament. In another chapter we will look again at these components and see how they relate to the bringing in of The New Covenant by Jesus Christ and the significance and links to the actions that took place in the concluding days of the ministry of Jesus whilst here on earth. It should also be noted that as we further consider the writings of the Apostles, as well as the teachings of Jesus, the relationship to the Covenant and its symbolism enriches God's great Plan of Salvation for mankind.

1. <u>Exchange of Coats</u>

The exchanging of gifts in the heathenistc ceremony is understood to be of a wide possibility, and could be of either livestock, precious material goods, or something of cultural significance. In the Hebrew/Biblical ceremony, this s confined to two elements of the ceremony, the first of which is to exchange coats. The significance of this is that the coat speaks of the personality and life of the individual, a type of physical covering of the body, but is here symbolically used to speak of a much deeper interchange bearing the same level of commitment and solemnity as that used in the heathenistic ceremony. In 1 Samuel 18:4a, *"Then the king said to them, "Whatever seems best to you I will do…"*, where David and Jonathan were coming into covenant, then the coat or the robe is shown to be the first part of the ceremony enacted between them. It should be noted that this Biblical record does not indicate the presence of a priest or holy man but in verse 3 clearly states that Jonathan was making a covenant with David: *"But the people answered, "You shall not go out! For if we flee away, they will not care about* us; *nor if half of us die, will they care about us. But you are worth ten thousand of us now. For you are now more help to us in the city."* It is assumed that, in this instance, with the absence of a priest it was made in an open confession, each to the other, before Almighty God and that the parties concerned operated at the level of solemnity and commitment as if a priest had been present.

2. <u>Exchange of Belts</u>

Throughout the ages, the belt around the midriff of a soldier has always been a store of weaponry, and the means by which weapons were suspended. Indeed, the modern soldier of today still uses his belt as an anchorage for such weaponry as hand weapons, hand grenades, ammunition and water flask, etc. The exchange of belts, therefore, with the weaponry they contained was more than symbolic. Not only did it enact the commitment of one party to the other, saying "All your weapons are at my disposal and all my weapons are at your disposal", but here is also the first instalment on such a commitment. We see that this happened between David and Jonathan, as recorded in I Samuel 18:4: *"And Jonathan stripped himself of the robe that was upon him, and gave it to David, and his armour and even his sword and his bow and his girdle."* In the first two parts of the ceremony that we have listed, there is a total and absolute commitment on each of the parties to cherish and support each other in a time of peace and war!

3. <u>Cut the Covenant and The Covenant Walk</u>

In this part of the ceremony, we have recorded for us in Genesis chapter 15, a most amazing story! It tells of the cutting of covenant between Abram and the Lord God Almighty. In order to understand it, we must first understand the significance of the sacrifice element of covenant that we described earlier, i.e. that an innocent animal's blood is shed, or in this case a series of animals' blood is shed, and the parties coming into covenant are identified with such a process. This truly is the heart of Biblical Blood Covenant. In Genesis 15:9,10 and 17-21, we have recorded for us the requirements of the cutting of covenant between Abram and the Lord God Almighty: *"So He said to him, 'Bring me a three year old heifer, a three year old female goat, a three year old ram, a turtledove, and a young pigeon.' Then he brought all these to Him and cut them in two, down the middle, and placed each piece opposite the other; but he did not cut the birds in two."* *"And it came to pass, when the sun went down and it was dark, that behold, there appeared a smoking oven and a burning torch that passed between those pieces. On the same day the Lord made a covenant with Abram, saying 'To your descendants I have given this land, from the river of Egypt to the great river, the River Euphrates—the Kenites, the Kenezzites, the Kadmonites, the Hittites, the Perizzites, the Rephaim, the Amorites, the Canaanites, the Girgashites, and the Jebusites.'"*

It may be worthwhile at this point, breaking into this element of the covenant ceremony, to consider the backdrop to this component recorded in Genesis 15. In Genesis 14, we have one of the most amazing stories of the Old Testament which is little known or appreciated by most Bible students. It may be worthwhile for you to break off reading this book at this time in order to read the story of Genesis 14. At the outset of the chapter, we have an alliance of kings who decided to rebel against a further alliance of kings from the north, Babylonia and Southern Assyria. We also have the involvement of Lot who broke away from Abram at an earlier stage, as described in Geneses Chapter 13, and settled in the city areas of Sodom and Gomorrah. Lot was taken prisoner by these armies from the north, which at that time must have been considered to be the best fighting machine in that part of the Middle East. This is demonstrated for us in the mop up exercise and return to payment of tithes and tribute to the northern kingdoms. The spiritual significance of the activities of Lot in this story is the key to the involvement of Almighty God fighting on behalf of Abram and his household army. Clearly, Abram had some sort of alliance with Eschol, Mamre and Anar. Genesis Chapter 14:14 clearly shows that when Abram went to war to rescue his nephew, the 318 men were household born and trained by Abram. *"Now when Abram heard that* his *brother was taken captive, he armed his three hundred and eighteen trained servants who were born in his own house, and went in pursuit as far as Dan."*

The next part of Genesis Chapter 14 tells the amazing story of how 318 men, in a pincer movement, defeated the greatest fighting machine of the Middle East, and routed and pursued them to Hobah, bringing back captive all their spoils. The likelihood of such military success can only be expressed in the terms of "a nonsense", when considered from a natural viewpoint, but the key to the whole thing is revealed by the appearing of Melchizedek who was priest of God Most High (verse 18). Here before the King of Sodom as witness, he blesses Abram and brings out bread and wine, which are covenant meal elements, and declares that Abram is blessed by God Most High who has delivered his enemies into his hand; thus, we have prior to the "cutting of the covenant" between Abram and The Lord God Almighty in Genesis Chapter 15, the fulfilment of several parts of a covenant ceremony by the priest of God Most High who appears unannounced on the scene and vanishes in similar manner.

It should be noted, that it is at this part of the ceremony, that Abram's response to Melchizedek is to give him a tithe of everything; therefore the practice of tithing to covenant between God and man is established at this time, and does not arise from Mosaic Law as many believe. It is true, however, that Mosaic Law enshrined the tithe for specific purposes, i.e. of sustaining the work of the priesthood, and the maintenance of The Tabernacle, and later, the Temple. It should also be noted, that the response that Abram gave to the King of Sodom with this part of the ceremony backdrop, is that he will have absolutely nothing to do with retaining the slightest material aspect that could be said to have belonged to the King of Sodom, not even the spoils of war given to Abram by the Lord God Almighty, so that the Name of the Lord God Almighty should in no way be connected to the King of Sodom. The only thing he retains to himself is the food for his fighting men, letting Anar, Eschol and Mamre take their share of the spoils.

The backdrop to Genesis Chapter 15 of the cutting of covenant is the proving by God Most High, of Abram, as a worthy partner with whom to relate in covenant. In the opening verses of Genesis Chapter 15, we see the exchange of the discussion, effectively "the terms of covenant" and "the promises" made to him by the Lord, and in Genesis 15:6, *"And he believed in the Lord, and He accounted it to him for righteousness."* We see the key to all covenants in that here Abram believes what God has said, and it is counted to him as righteousness, i.e. faith has to be declared each to the other as the basis of covenant. From this point on in Genesis Chapter 15, the Lord identifies Himself as Who He Is and asks Abram to lay out the sacrifice of the covenant, a 3-year-old heifer, a 3-year-old she goat, a 3-year-old ram, a turtle dove and a young pigeon. Here, we see the covenant sacrifice of these animals. They are cut in two, separated by a pathway, with the exception of the birds, and Abram has to defend these sacrifices all day against the birds of prey that want to come and take them away. Here again, we see in this aspect, the symbolism of the birds of prey trying to destroy the bringing in of the covenant, the blessing that is going to be through Abram to all the nations of the world.

Whilst Genesis 15 shows the cutting of the covenant, the Genesis account is a very special account, because Almighty God does not reveal Himself to partake in this part of the covenant as a human being. In a normal cutting of covenant ceremony the priest would be present and the two parties would hold hands and walk together down the pathway between the halved bodies of the animals and birds. The "covenant walk", as it is referred to, is obliquely referred to in Amos 3:3, where we read, *"Can two walk together unless they are agreed?"* (KJV).

In this instance, we have the two parties involved in various time frames. Abram defends the sacrifice all day, driving off the birds of prey, and at eventide a deep sleep and darkness falls upon him. The Lord God Almighty brings forth further promises of a prophetic nature regarding the offspring that will yet appear, and when the sun is fully down and the darkness appears, the smoking firepot and the flaming torch are seen to pass between the pieces of the sacrifice (Genesis 15:17): *"And it came to pass, when the sun went down and it was dark, that behold, there appeared a smoking oven and a burning torch that passed between those pieces."* It is thought by some that these two symbols had their origins in Ur of the Chaldees where Abram was raised, and that they were used here to identify to Abram that he was dealing with the Almighty God. In Genesis 15:18-20, the Lord God Almighty declares a covenant is made with Abram, and the land that is pledged to Abram's descendants is clearly defined: *"On the same day the Lord made a covenant with Abram, saying, "To your descendents I have given this land, from the river of Egypt to the great river, the River Euphrates—the Kenites, the Kenezzites, the Kadmonites, the Hittites, the Perizzites, the Rephaim, the Amonites, the Canaanites, the Girqashites, and the Jebusites."* In modern-day parlance, this reaches from the River Nile in Egypt to the River Euphrates, in modern-day Iraq and Iran.

4. <u>Exchange of Names</u>

Having come into covenant and passed the cutting element, the last exchange part of this ceremony now takes place. We have seen in Steps 1 and 2, the exchange of the very life and personality of the individuals concerned together with their weaponry and armour exchange. This now brings us to the third element in this exchange. In order to understand this, we must first understand that in Middle East culture, in Biblical times, and to some extent still today, when a new born child was named it was of more significance and involvement than the mere whim of the parents. Family characteristics and events surrounding the birth of the new born child would be enshrined in the naming of the child; therefore, in a covenant ceremony when there was an exchange of names it spoke both of the nature and characteristic of the individual and the family history that had brought that individual to the point of covenant.

In Genesis 17, we have the making of further covenant between Abram and God Almighty, with promises and exchange, showing that this covenant is an Everlasting Covenant regarding possession and that Almighty God will be his God forever and the God of his descendants.

In Genesis 17:5 and 15, *"No longer shall your name be called Abram, but your name shall be Abraham; for I have made you a father of many nations."* Then God said to Abraham, *"As for Sarai your wife, you shall not call her name Sarai, but Sarah shall be her name."* We have the exchange of names, in that "ah" is interjected into the middle of Abram which becomes Abraham, and the same "ah" is added to Sarai and the "ai" dropped so that her name becomes Sarah. The origins of this part of the Name of God are thought to come from either Jehovah or Yahweh and are now part of both Abraham and Sarah's names equally. When addressed, Sarah has difficulty in accepting that she will become a mother due to her age.

In this covenant ceremony recorded in Genesis 17, we also see "the sign" of covenant by circumcision taking a significant place in Middle East culture of the time, and even today. Circumcision was practised for medical and hygiene reasons and here we see a common practice being adopted. So serious is this part of the ceremony that the Lord God declares that those who do not have this sign in their flesh are to be cut off from His people as they are considered to have broken covenant.

5. Making a Scar

In this element of the *Hebrew/Biblical* ceremony, a critical difference of practice between this and the heathenistic covenant ceremony takes place. As discussed in the previous chapter, the heathenistic ceremony involved the physical consumption of human blood into the digestive tract by drinking from the cup of wine with blood mingled into it. Here a scar is made which would draw blood, usually on the palm of the right hand. This would be done as a permanent testifier to the covenant in the bodies of the participants.

In Isaiah 49:16, the prophet is imploring Zion regarding the promises that have been made, and compares a mother's forgetfulness for her child as a possibility, but not so with the Lord since the prophet says, *"See, I have inscribed you on the palms of My hands; your walls are continually before Me."* This is a direct reference by the Living God, through the prophet, to tell His people that the scar mark on the palms of the hands is a permanent reminder and testifier to the covenant status. Here, the prophet is chiding Zion for their forgetfulness, and their breaking of covenant.

Jesus reminds Thomas of His Resurrection in John 20:24-29: *"Now Thomas, called the Twin, one of the twelve, was not with them when Jesus came. The other disciples therefore* said *to him, 'We have seen the Lord.' So he said to them, 'Unless I see in His hands the print of the nails, and put my* finger *into the print of the nails, and put my hand into His side, I will not believe.'"* The scars in His Body made by the nails and the sword, and these scar marks were sufficient to completely break Thomas and cause him to be restored in his faith in Jesus, as both his Lord and his God. It is also said by some that many Jewish mothers would make a scar on their hands as a reminder of the children they had birthed in the marriage, as they went about their daily home duties

6. Striking of Hands

This part of the ceremony was when the two right hands of the individuals who had just had a scar made on them would be grasped in a similar manner as when we today would shake hands with someone to whom we were being introduced. It is all part and parcel of the ceremony leading to the ultimate state of friendship. In this act, the life blood of the two individuals would be intermingled as both palms would be bloody and it showed an expression of the exchange of life between the participants. In Leviticus 17:11 and 14, the Mosaic law is quite clear about the life of the flesh being in the blood. Here we see in verse 11, *"For the life of the flesh is in the blood, and I have given it to you upon the altar to make atonement for your souls; for it is the blood that makes atonement for the soul."* *"For it is the life of all flesh. Its blood sustains its life. Therefore I said to the children of Israel, "You shall not eat the blood of any flesh, for the life of all flesh is in its blood. Whoever eats it shall be cut off."* It has been given for the making of atonement because of the life of the creature. You will also see from verse 10 of that same chapter that anyone of the house of Israel, or stranger who lived among them, who ate any blood would have the Face of God set against him, and he would be cut off from among God's people. *"And whatever man of the house of Israel, or of the stranger who dwell among you, who eats any blood, I will set My face against that person who eats blood, and will cut him off from among his people."* For this reason, the cup of wine that will subsequently be used in this ceremony does not have any human or other blood intermingled with it but the cup of wine remains a symbolic form only of the drinking of blood.

7. The Giving of Terms

We have covered this aspect in the previous chapter and have shown it to be part of the larger section of a covenant ceremony that is involved in the promise section. To remind the reader, we have said that in a heathenistic covenant the terms of the covenant could list the dire consequences of breaking of covenant, and the enactment of consequent curses of a both specific and general nature. Often such curses would revolve around the bringing on of infertility to the people and animals of the tribe or nation.

In the Hebrew/Biblical covenant terms there are many examples in Scripture that are given to us. We have already looked at Genesis 15 and 17, where the terms allied to each covenant are quite clearly stated. These are inevitably given in a promise where the Lord says, "I will…" and some particular action on God's part is committed to being brought about to the increase and blessing of Abram and Sarai in their new state as Abraham and Sarah

One of the most often quoted passages of scripture relating to the blessings of covenant is that of Deuteronomy 28, and sadly at many of the meetings where I have heard this passage read, there have been significant omissions and only part reading of the chapter, so as to present a totally lopsided case. If you read the passage fully from the beginning at verse 1, "*Now it shall come to pass, if you diligently obey the voice of the Lord your God, to observe carefully all His* commandments *which I command you today, that the Lord* your *God will set you high above all nations of the earth."* There is a very clear condition of requirement for the blessings to be enacted, which is the full obedience to the Voice of the Lord God and the blessings that are subsequently listed in the first fourteen verses of that chapter are subsequently repeated as curses upon those who disobey the Voice of the Lord. Indeed, by far the larger portion of the rest of that chapter talks of the curses for those who are disobedient. It should be noted that whilst there is no covenant ceremony specifically mentioned here as having taken place in chapter 28, it is the teaching of the Law of God through Moses, and the expansion of such covenant promises and warnings to the people to obey the requirements of God's Laws if they wish to know the blessings of the Lord in their lives both as individuals as well as a nation.

This section of the covenant ceremony is the core of the outworking of covenant and it will test our obedience and faith in our God. Subsequent stories are recorded for us particularly in the Old Testament Scriptures, where one person disobeying the commandment of the Lord, brings dire consequences on the whole nation, thus showing the need for all of God's people to be obedient in covenant matters. Examples of this happening are recorded with characters such as Achan and Korah bringing disastrous consequences on other people as well as themselves.

8. Eat a Memorial Meal

In order to support God's laws and standards in a covenant ceremony, the use of bread and wine to symbolise sacrifices of the ceremony, i.e. the slaughtered innocent animals, then bread and wine as a minimum memorial meal were used, with bread signifying the flesh of the animals and wine the blood of the animals. Genesis 49:11: *"Binding his donkey to the vine, and his donkey's colt to the choice vine, he washed his garments in wine and his clothes in the blood of grapes."* And Deuteronomy 32:14: *"Curds from the cattle and milk of the flock with fat of lambs; and rams of the breed of Bashan and goats, with the choicest wheat; and you drank wine, the blood of grapes."* Both clarify that wine is considered as the blood of the grape, hence the use of wine as a symbol of blood; also Leviticus 17:11 confirms the principle that there is *"life in the blood"*.

In Genesis 14:18, *"Then Melchizedek king of Salem brought out bread and wine; he was the priest of God Most High.",* referred to earlier, the priest Melchisedek brought forth bread and wine, and proceeded to bless Abram; thus the covenant meal element was produced prior to the major happening in Genesis Chapter 15.

When Jesus inaugurated The New Covenant in what we know as The Last Supper, as recorded for us in Luke 22:14-20, *"When the hour had come, He sat down, and the twelve apostles with Him. Then He said to them, 'With fervent desire I have desired to eat this Passover with you before I suffer; for I say to you, I will no longer eat of it until it is fulfilled in the kingdom of God.' Then He took the cup, and gave thanks, and said, 'Take this and divide it among yourselves, for I say to you, I will not drink of the fruit of the vine until the kingdom of God comes.' And He took bread, gave thanks and broke it, and gave to them saying, 'This is My body which is given for you; do this in remembrance of Me.'"* The Jewish disciples who met around that table were clear in their own minds and thinking because of their Jewish upbringing, that when Jesus took the cup and then took the bread and blessed it and shared it with them, He was actually lifting this element from a Blood Covenant ceremony to the elevated position of a memorial feast of great symbolism and significance, and would not have needed to explain to these disciples the significance of His actions.

Whilst other gospels record this event prior to Jesus crucifixion, Dr Luke records for us the fuller activity and significance of that meal in covenant terms, in that Jesus refers in Luke 22:20, to the Cup which is poured out being the New Covenant in His Blood. *"Likewise He also took the cup after supper,* saying, *'This cup is the new covenant in My blood, which is shed for you.'"* In similar manner in verse 19, He takes bread and breaks it and refers to it as His Body being given for them. *"And He took the bread, gave thanks and broke it, and gave it to them saying, 'This is My body which is given for you; do this in remembrance of Me.'"* Theologians over many generations have struggled with these Scriptures and have brought forth, what I believe to be wrong doctrine, in the use of bread and wine. The reason for this is very simple. If the individual would appreciate that the memorial feast that Jesus blessed and asked to be a memorial for Him was lifted straight from the Blood Covenant ceremony of eating a memorial meal using bread and wine as symbols of flesh and blood, and the commitment to each of the parties in such an act, the whole issue of using bread as a substitute for the flesh, and wine as a substitute for the blood in the Blood Covenant Ceremony is clarified. It is surely in obedience to God's standards which were later clarified by the giving of the Law by Moses that is that Melchisedek, priest of God Most High, used these elements in the covenant linked ceremony to God and Abram coming into covenant, and in the same way Jesus has used these same elements of bread and wine, to be used as a memorial feast until He comes again, as a reminder of The New Covenant which He has brought as a restoration of the original relationship between God and Man at the original creation time.

9. <u>Plant a Tree</u>

Whilst there are several reminders and testifiers in the elements of the ceremony covered so far, it was always intended that the covenant should be recorded in some way in the earth, by a permanent witness to all. In Genesis 21:32 and 33, we see the conclusion of a covenant ceremony between Abimelech and Abraham. *"Thus they* made a *covenant at Beersheba. So Abimelech rose with Phicol, the commander of his army, and they returned to the land of the Philistines. Then Abraham planted a tamarisk tree in Beersheba, and there called on the name of the Lord, the Everlasting God."* We see in the story the account in verses 25-34, *"Then Abraham rebuked Abimelech because of a well of water which Abimelech's servants had seized, And Abimelech said, 'I do not know who has done this thing; you did not tell me, nor had I heard of it until today'."* So Abraham took sheep and oxen and gave them to Ahimelech, and the two of them made a covenant. And Abraham set seven ewe lambs of the flock by themselves. Then Abimelech asked Abraham, 'What is the meaning of these seven ewe lambs which you have set by themselves?' And he said, 'You will take* these *seven ewe lambs from my hand, that they be my witnesses that I have dug this well.' Therefore he called that place Beersheba. So Abimelech rose with Phicol, the commander of his army, and they returned to the land of the Philistines. Then Abra-*

ham planted a tamarisk tree in Beersheba, and there called on the name of the Lord, the Everlasting God. And Abraham stayed in the land of the Philistines many days." Here are witnesses recorded in the ceremony e.g. verse 30 refers to seven ewe lambs which would continue the witness down their generations, but that Abraham plants a Tamarisk Tree and calls on the Name of the Lord, the Everlasting God, as an additional part of the ceremony after Abimelech and the Philistines have departed. The planting and growing of a tree is a wooden signifier to the covenant that had taken place and in the New Covenant brought in by Jesus. The permanent witness the world over to that covenant, is a Cross—being a wooden tree on which Jesus was crucified. Of course, it is not always possible to plant a tree in some parts of the earth as the ground will not support the growth of vegetation and trees, particularity in arid climates. Where this is the case, there has often been a single stone or a heap of stones raised up as a pillar to signify the site at which the covenant took place; and, indeed, Scripture also uses this means of a permanent testifier to record the siting of other major significant events. Down the centuries of time, stones of various shapes with inscriptions have been the last witness to the existence of individuals, whether in a graveyard, or a plaque in some significant place. We see this same idea as a means of witness throughout the generations of mankind.

Questions on Chapter 4

1. List 3 elements or stages of the Biblical Blood Covenant that refer directly or indirectly to the concept of an exchange of life, nature or characteristic of the parties coming into covenant.

2. Relative to the above, read through the passages of Scripture discussed for these 3 stages and research other Biblical references that you feel cover these same aspects.

3. What is the main important difference with the use of blood between a heathenistic covenant ceremony and a Hebrew/Biblical covenant ceremony?

4. Relative to (3) above, list and read the Scriptures that support the use of blood in this context, and see if you can find other Scripture that supports the same viewpoint.

5. With the exchange of belts there was symbolism of great significance regarding what aspect? How would this affect (a) two individuals, (b) a small group or tribe and (c) a full nation?

6. In the making of a scar in the flesh as a permanent testifier to the event, what scars may have been seen in the Philistine champion story of I Samuel 17 as compared to the scars spoken of by the prophet Isaiah in Isaiah 49.16?

7. In the giving of terms of the covenant, contrast the difference of this part of the ceremony between heathenistic and Hebrew/Biblical. List 3 different aspects likely to be covered in such terms of the Biblical/Blood Covenant.

8. In the eating of a memorial meal (a) what symbols were used and what did they represent? (b) When these same symbols were used by Jesus, why did He give no explanation or interpretation of them to the assembled disciples?

9. Why was a tree or a pile of stones or a single stone used at the end of the ceremony?

10. Relative to Question 9, why is something to do with the Christian Religion associated with the symbol of a cross?

5

THE ULTIMATE BLOOD COVENANT RELATIONSHIP

In our thoughts so far, we have considered in quite some depth, the various stages of both heathenistic and Hebrew/Biblical covenant ceremonies. We have shown that in both these ceremonies, when completed in the presence of a religious representative such as a priest or witch doctor or juju man or similar, that both these ceremonies bring parties together either directly or through their representatives, into a state to which both have committed themselves under the highest possible authority that they relate to, and in that state they have a special relationship of utter commitment and dependency. For individuals this status is called friendship. For groups, be they small or large, other words tend to be used such as "an alliance" or "league". It will be seen that several other words are readily generated from this status to cover this concept of commitment, even to our modern society; thus we have phrases like "the League of Nations", "the Commonwealth of Nations" and many Charitable Bodies or objects of mercy such as hospitals which are supported by a group known as "the friends of…", whatever is the name of the charitable organisation or object. Indeed, this latter phrase can be used as a support group to a particular religious ministry or similar, generating support at international or local levels.

The information that we have given so far would be of little or no worth if it were to be left hanging at this stage. It may be of interest to some, and annoyance to others, and the book would not be worth writing were it to terminate here without showing the great application of this process that has been brought into being between Heaven and Earth and the relationship in covenant that our Great God has devised using this system that is universally understood and practised from the early days of primitive society to this present time, even if sadly, in our sophisticated New Millennium, our western ways of sophistication seem to have bypassed, to our great cost, the understanding of this basic relationship

From the beginning of the Biblical account there are more than straws in the wind to show that God relates to His people through the relationship of covenant. Sometimes there are strong hints or direct records that would tell us that the Biblical account is either based on or referring to the idea or concept enshrined in Biblical Blood Covenant. For instance, in the Creation Story we have an open relationship and conversation between God and man. Genesis 2:15-17 records such a conversation: *"Then the Lord God took the man and put him in* the *garden of Eden to tend and keep it. And the Lord God commanded the man, saying, 'Of every tree of the garden you may freely eat'"*, and at the Fall of Man as recorded in Genesis 3, and the coming of sin, we see in verse 21 that it was a covering of skins that Adam and his wife were provided with: *"And for Adam and his wife, the Lord God made tunics of skin and clothed them."* We can safely conclude from this record that the skins at one time belonged to animals that had given their lives for such a covering. It is generally accepted, even back to this record, that the shedding of blood is necessary for the covering of sin or atonement as the Scripture records. The Law given by God to Moses and the subsequent introduction of the Tabernacle Sacrifice System enshrines this basic use of blood for the covering or atonement for the sin of man by the use of the shedding of blood of the innocent animal. Indeed, the use of blood and sprinkling of sacrificial animal blood plays a key factor in the ceremonies of The Tabernacle and later Temple, together with the purifying of objects and the bringing in of priests to their rank and office under the Old Testament Covenant.

With this in mind, we will now show the links between God's Plan of Salvation and how this was fulfilled based on the requirements of the Blood Covenant Ceremony that we have just discussed. While it may appear to be repetitious, I ask the reader to bear with me, and see the striking fulfilment that Jesus brought into the earth by His appearing, by His ministry, and by His subsequent death and resurrection and ascension into the Heavenlies on our behalf.

A summary of these points and references are shown for you in tables on pages 38-39.

Step 1—Exchange of Coats

We saw that the exchange of coats signified the exchange of the life and the personality coming into covenant in symbolic form. In John 3:5-7, *"Jesus answered, 'Most assuredly I say to you, unless one is born of water and the Spirit, he cannot enter the kingdom of God. That which is born of the flesh is flesh, and that which is born of the Spirit is spirit. Do not marvel that I said to you, "You* must be *born again."* Jesus is teaching the necessity for the new birth and we know that in our salvation there is a work done in us by The Holy Spirit whereby we are "born again of the Holy Spirit of God", i.e. we become regenerate. The Holy Spirit of God comes and indwells us. Truly, in our salvation this part of a Blood Covenant becomes a living reality.

Step 2—Exchange of Belts

The weaponry that becomes available to us and is at our disposal is an absolute necessity if the Christian is going to survive the Christian walk. From our initial salvation just discussed, it is of the utmost importance that we understand that to become a Christian we must undergo a spiritual process, a work of the Holy Spirit, a regeneration of our own spirit by such heavenly interaction. If we fail to understand this fundamental characteristic of Christian life, we will remain easy meat for Satan and his agents to tempt us, and for us to fall to that temptation and into sin. Our God is faithful in providing us with weapons that are spiritual and available to every Christian born again of the Spirit of God! The weaponry that is available to us is spoken of many times in the New Testament, both by Jesus and also in the apostolic writings of The Epistles.

In John 16, Jesus is teaching on the coming to earth of the Holy Spirit in place of Himself when He will no longer be in the earth. In verses 23 and 24 of that chapter, Jesus tells us that if we ask anything of the Father in His Name, it will be given to us. *"And in that day you will ask Me nothing. Most assuredly I say to you, whatever you ask the Father in My name He will give you. Until now you have asked nothing in My name. Ask and you will receive, that your joy may be full."* He encourages us to ask so that we may receive so that our joy may be full. This gives us the authority to ask The Father in the Name of Jesus for any weaponry or any supporting heavenly army we may need to act on our behalf in any particular set of circumstances. There is much to be said, and books have been written on this subject alone, but this holy access to the throne room of heaven is no place for either flippancy, material greed or abuse. Our covenant is too solemn for much that passes in the use of the Name of Jesus in some parts of the Church today.

The Apostle Paul, in writing to the Church at Ephesus in Ephesians 6:10-20, uses what is thought to be a parallel example based on the armour of a Roman soldier, and all the pieces of the armour that are at our disposal calling it "The Armour of God". *"Finally, my brethren, be strong in the Lord and in the power of*

His might. Put on the whole armour of God, that you may be able to stand against the wiles of the devil. For we do not wrestle against flesh and blood, but against powers, against the rulers of the darkness of this age, against spiritual hosts of wickedness in the heavenly places. Therefore take up the whole armour of God, that you may be able to withstand in the evil day, and having done all to stand. Stand therefore, having girded your waist with truth, having put on the breastplate of righteousness, and having shod your feet with the preparation of the gospel of peace; above all, taking the shield of faith with which you will be able to quench all the fiery darts of the wicked one. And take the helmet of salvation, and the sword of the Spirit, which is the word of God; praying always with all prayer and supplication in the Spirit, being watchful to this end with all perseverance and supplication for all the saints and for me, that utterance may be given to me, that I may open my mouth boldly to make known the mystery of the gospel for which I am an ambassador in chains; that in it I may speak boldly, as I ought to speak." He encourages us at the outset in verse 10, to be strong in the Lord and in the strength of HIS might! He also tells us to put on the WHOLE armour, so that we can stand against the wiles of the devil, and he proceeds to list out SEVEN pieces of armour that will strengthen us. Here I would point out that many commentators have missed the seventh piece of armour, and I suggest the reason is that the Roman soldier did not have a piece of armour quite like it. In verse 12, Paul clearly teaches that we are not contending against mere flesh and blood, but against the spiritual powers that have various levels of power, and these are listed for us. He speaks of the principalities and is very much against these powers. He speaks of world rulers, he speaks of spiritual hosts of wickedness in heavenly places, and before listing out for us the SEVEN-piece armour of God, he is clearly defining that these things are in the spiritual realm and not in the natural realm. Once again, we have to refer back to the spiritual experience that is necessary for a person to become a Christian. If we remain in our natural state of mind we will have no understanding of the spiritual standing and significance of the weaponry that is available to us. He speaks of truth in the midriff, he speaks of the breastplate of righteousness covering the heart of the individual, he speaks of our feet being shod with the equipment of the gospel of peace, he speaks of the shield of faith being able to quench ALL the fiery darts of the evil one, The Roman shield was a major piece of warfare equipment and the Roman soldiers were taught how to use it to very great effect in covering themselves, and joining with others, in making major attacks into enemy strongholds and cities. He identifies the sword of the Spirit as the Word of God, which we would recognise as the Scripture, and lastly but by no means least, in verse 18 he refers to praying in the Spirit at all times. This last great weapon, praying in the language of the Holy Spirit, is a very powerful weapon. For some, they mock it, for others they try not to believe in it, and yet others try to make it something of controversial debate. You may draw for yourself any conclusion as to why this seventh weapon of the Christian had no likeness in a mere Roman armoury. My experience of its use has stood me in good stead through many situations and over many years and the experience of its use surpasses debate.

For the reader there is much that can be gained from the study of the Scriptures listed in this section.

Step 3—The Cutting of the Covenant

The validity in history of the work of Jesus and His appearing in history is so important that our calendars are set by it, despite the effort of modern scholars to try and rewrite history and take its dating away from anno domini and before Christ.

In his first letter to the Corinthian Church, chapter 5:6-8, *"Your glorying is not good. Do you not know that a little leaven leavens the whole lump? Therefore purge out the old leaven, that you may be a new lump, since you truly are unleavened. For indeed Christ, our Passover, was sacrificed for* us. *Therefore let us keep the feast, not with old leaven, nor with the leaven of malice and wickedness, but with the unleavened bread of sincerity and truth."* Paul is disciplining the members of the Church in relation to immoral practices, and pronouncing judgement on them, and in the latter part of verse seven as the lynch pin of his argument, states that Christ our Paschal Lamb, has been sacrificed. Here, the term "Paschal Lamb" is a direct reference to the lambs killed in remembrance of the great deliverance from Egypt of God's people, and is celebrated in the Feast of the Passover. Here, the lambs' lives were taken and the blood sprinkled over the doorpost of each household, as a means of deliverance out of Egypt and the power of the occult gods that Egypt represented. In referring to Jesus Christ as a Paschal Lamb, the apostle is clearly identifying that when Christ was crucified and His body pierced with a spear, He was the ultimate sacrifice for us in bringing in The New Covenant. The Apostle Peter confirms this argument in 1 Peter 1:18-20: *"…knowing that you were not redeemed with corruptible things like silver or gold, from your aimless conduct received by tradition from your fathers, but with the precious blood of Christ, as of a lamb without blemish and without spot. He indeed was foreordained before the foundation of the world, but was manifest in these last times for you."* He likens the Precious Blood of Christ to that of a lamb without spot or blemish. He also confirms at the end of that passage, that this was no mistake or misjudgement on the part of man, but it was the Plan of God right from the foundation of the world; therefore, we have in this step also all the requirements for a covenant sacrifice on the part of the innocent animal.

Step 4—Exchange of Names

When we consider this step it gives one of the strongest indications that the bringing in of The New Covenant by Jesus Christ was truly a Blood Covenant. Also, as has been listed—where there are several stages of the ceremony which do not necessarily all occur at the same point in time, so also we have a similar thing happening here.

The Apostle Peter, in his first Epistle, is clearly identifying in chapter 4:16, that there is absolutely no shame whatsoever in being referred to as "a Christian", but rather that under that Name we should glorify God. "*Yet if anyone suffers as a Christian, let him not be ashamed, but let him glorify God in this matter.*"

We know from the Book of Acts, the name "Christian" clearly identified a person as a follower of Jesus Christ, and they were first called Christians at Antioch, Acts 11:26. "*And when he had found him, he brought him to Antioch. So it was that for a whole year they assembled with the church and taught a great many people. And the disciples were first called Christians in Antioch.*" King Agrippa was today insulted at the thought that he might even be referred to as a Christian by the persuasion of Paul.

The Jews referred to their expected Redeemer as "Messiah". To the Gentiles, He is referred to as Christ; therefore the term "Christian" signifies a follower of Jesus Christ and truly fulfils that step of the covenant ceremony. Also, in being referred to as "Christian" and bearing in mind that Biblical names display the characteristic of the person, the Apostle Paul in Galatians 5:15-26, encourages us to bring forth the fruit of the Spirit. "*But if you bite and devour one another, beware lest you be consumed by one another! I say then: Walk in the Spirit, and you shall not fulfil the lusts of the flesh. For if the flesh lusts against the Spirit, and the Spirit against the flesh; and these are contrary to one another, so that you do not do the things that you wish. But if you are led by the Spirit you are not under the law. Now the works of the flesh are evident, which are: adultery, fornication, uncleanness, lewdness, idolatry, sorcery, hatred, contentions, jealousies, outbursts of wrath, selfish ambitions, dissensions, heresies, envy, murders, drunkenness, revelries and the like; of which I tell you beforehand, just as I told you in time past, that those who practice such things will not inherit the kingdom of God. But the fruit of the Spirit is love, joy, peace, longsuffering, kindness, goodness, faithfulness, gentleness, self-control. Against such there is no law. And those who are Christ's have crucified the flesh with its passions and desires. If we live in the Spirit, let us also walk in the Spirit. Let us not become conceited, provoking one another, envying one another."* He also lists in sharp contrast the characteristics of the works of the flesh and concludes his instruction that those who belong to Christ Jesus have crucified the flesh with its passions and desires. I wonder how many of us can identify with this characteristic exchange as well as being called Christian?

Step 5—Striking the Hands

The striking of the hands has always been a sign of agreement between parties, not only in Old Testament Biblical times, but also in the handshake of today indicating the sign of welcome on a peaceful basis.

In Biblical times the striking of the hand also indicated a sign of business agreement of a deal where the taking off of the shoe or sandal was deemed to be an equivalent procedure such as is recorded in the Book of Ruth 4:7-8. *"Now this was the custom in former times in Israel concerning redeeming and exchanging, to confirm anything; one man took off his sandal and gave it to the other, and this was confirmation in Israel. Therefore the close relative said to Boaz, 'Buy it for yourself.' So he took off his sandal."* It is interesting to note that in this instance, the raising up of heritage and continuation of generational issue, is the matter under discussion.

With the covenant striking or shaking of hands, because there would be a scar on the palm of each hand, it also spoke of the literal mixing of the blood in the two blooded hands, which was the literal mixing of life, as we have shown already that blood signifies the life.

In the New Covenant, we have an amazing story of the mixing of blood between Heaven and Earth. In Luke's gospel account, bearing in mind that Luke was a medical doctor of his day, we have the amazing story of how Mary, a virgin, becomes pregnant and ultimately brings forth a Child called Jesus. The key to this process is recorded in Luke 1:35, where we are told that the work of the Holy Spirit will both come upon her and overshadow her, and that the resulting Child would be called Holy and the Son of God. *"And the angel answered and said to her, 'The Holy Spirit will come upon you, and the power of the Highest will overshadow you; therefore, also, that Holy One who is to be born will be called the Son of*

God.'" As time has progressed, the covenant significance of this pregnancy in common with all other pregnancies, is that the God ordained natural process in the womb of a woman in bringing forth a child to the point of birth is such, that the blood system of the embryo and subsequent child is totally independent of the mother, and is a logical consequence of the parentage of the child to be born.

It is only in relatively modern times where scientific procedures have become available to us that the medical profession has reached the stage whereby the blood of a child, while still in the womb, can be changed because of the medical problems that it may produce when coming to birth and subsequently. We have clear scientific evidence that the blood of the child, being independent, and a logical consequence of its parentage, in the case of Jesus would be the result of the interaction between heaven and earth. Whilst it may have taken 2000 years or thereabouts to be able to apply the knowledge we have had for some time, it took the wisdom of Almighty God to so bring forth His Creation with the characteristic that in His foreknowledge the requirements of a Blood Covenant could have been enacted through a virgin birth where scriptural evidence is on record as to how Jesus was born and carried this blood in His Body for some 33 years, and was ultimately crucified, thus shedding this very special blood of covenant requirement down the Cross and into the earth.

My viewpoint on this matter relative to God's Plan of Salvation is simple but firm—no virgin birth, no sacrifice on Calvary, therefore no salvation. The mingling of blood as would have occurred in the striking of the hands as a step of the Biblical Blood Covenant Ceremony, in my opinion, takes on greater proportions of significance than those who argue over the resurrection of the Body of Jesus.

It is said by some, that to destroy the case for the resurrection of Jesus, is to destroy the case for the Christian Gospel as even Paul did in 1 Corinthians 15:12-22. *"Now if Christ is preached that He has been raised from the dead, how do some among you say that there is no resurrection from the dead? But if there is no resurrection of the dead, then Christ is not risen. And if Christ is not risen, then our preaching is empty and your faith is also empty. Yes, and we are found false witnesses of God, because we have testified of God that He raised up Christ, whom He did not raise up—if in fact the dead do not rise. For if the dead do not rise, then Christ is not risen. And if Christ is not risen, your faith is futile; you are still in your sins! Then also those who have fallen asleep in Christ have perished. If in this life only we have hope in Christ, we are of all men the most pitiable. But now Christ is risen from the dead, and has become the first fruits of those who have fallen* asleep. *For since by man came death, by Man also came the resurrection of the dead. For as in Adam all die, even so in Christ all shall be made alive. "* If there is no blood of significance or worth then The New Covenant fails with or without resurrection because the lynch pin of our salvation revolves around the Cross of Jesus at Calvary and His Work, and His Resurrection is a mere sign to the world and proof of heavenly declaration of the validity of The New Covenant. It is worth mentioning here, and drawing to your attention, the observation of the medical doctor and gospel writer, Dr. Luke, when in chapter 24:36-43, he describes to us an encounter with the Resurrected Christ and the discussion that took place as to what sort of a Body He had in Hs resurrected form. *"Now as they said these things, Jesus Himself stood in the midst of them, and said to them, 'Peace to you.' But they were terrified and frightened, and supposed they had seen a spirit. And He said to them, 'Why are you troubled? And why do doubts arise in your hearts? Behold My hands and My feet, that it is I Myself. Handle Me and see, for a spirit does not have flesh and bones as you see I have.' When He had said this, He showed them His hands and His feet. But while they still did not believe for joy, and marvelled, He said to them, 'Have you any food here?' So they gave Him a piece of a broiled fish, and some honeycomb. And He took it and ate in their presence."* Indeed, much discussion on this subject alone could be quite worthwhile, although nowhere in this post-resurrection account, nor in any other place in Scripture, to my knowledge, is any reference either directly or indirectly made of the significant non-recording of the Body of Jesus having any blood in the post-resurrection state. The reason for this is very simple in that the commission of Jesus was to come from Heaven into this world to bring in The New Covenant where the special blood generated through the virgin birth was to be contained in the special Body given to Him by the virgin birth and that Body served a specific purpose for some 33 years, and its purpose in that form was finalised and completed by the work on the Cross of Calvary, and the blood it contained remained in the earth when it was drained of all blood by the work of crucifixion and the execution squad. We will return to the significance of the blood of Jesus later when we consider the application of The New Covenant.

Step 6—Making the Scar

We have already considered that the heathenistic scars on the bodies of the participants served as a permanent testifier, and the use of blood through the incision was used in a very different manner. The scars received in the body of Jesus were used to great effect when Jesus dealt with one disciple alone, Thomas, when He invited him to see in His Hands the print of the nails, and to put his finger into their mark and also into His side where the spear had pierced. Here, Thomas saw for himself the reality of the signs that he had demanded as proof of the identity of the experience that Jesus had been through.

The Cross of Jesus is the sign today, the world over, of the work and message of the Christian Gospel and the scars that Jesus received on that Cross are recorded for us in John 20:27-29, *"Then He said to Thomas, 'Reach your finger here, and look at My hands; and reach your hand here, and put it into My side. Do not be unbelieving, but believing.' And Thomas answered and said to Him, 'My Lord and my God!' Jesus said to him, 'Thomas, because you have seen Me, you have believed. Blessed are those who have not seen and yet have believed.'"*

Step 7—Giving of Terms

Whilst in the general blood covenant ceremony, a sharp distinction is apparent between heathenistic and Hebrew/Biblical ceremonies, it is only in the light of The New Covenant, with its spiritual overtone and involvement in spiritual things, that we can examine the Giving of Terms in The New Covenant.

Already in Section 2 of this Chapter, we have seen and discussed the elements of exchange of weaponry at our disposal and indeed with the promises that Jesus made in His ministry, we need to be very clear of the spiritual worth of The New Covenant and its terms in application and in working out the Christian life. Paul, in writing in 2 Corinthians 8:9, *"For you know the grace of our Lord Jesus Christ, that though He was rich, yet for your* sakes *He became poor, that you through His poverty might become* rich…*"* and Ephesians 2:1-10, *"And you He made alive, who were dead in trespasses and sins, in which you once walked according to the* course *of this world, according to the prince of the power of the air, the spirit who now works in the sons of disobedience, among whom also we all once conducted ourselves in the lusts of our flesh, fulfilling the desires of the flesh and of the mind, and were by nature children of wrath, just as the others. But God, who is rich in mercy, because of His great love with which He loved us, even when we were dead in trespasses, made us alive together with Christ (by grace you have been saved), and raised us up together, and made us sit together in the heavenly places in Christ Jesus, that in the ages to come He might show the exceeding riches of His grace in His kindness toward us in Christ Jesus. For by grace you have been saved through faith, and that not of yourselves; it is the gift of God, not of works, lest anyone should boast. For we are His workmanship, created in Christ Jesus for good works, which God prepared beforehand that we should walk in them."* Paul clearly shows the exchange in assets brought about by the Promise of The Father (a New Testament term for The Holy Spirit) through the obedience of Jesus Christ in coming from the glory of heaven, carrying out His commission in the earth, and His returning into the heavenlies to the right hand of The Father. Indeed, if you read carefully the epistle of Paul to the Ephesian church, especially the first two chapters, you will find there is a major bible study to be had in identifying in the text as to who is being referred to in the many pronouns used to identify which is the work of The Father, which is the work of Christ and the relative position of the believer's interaction with both the Father and Christ Jesus. Spiritual maturity is necessary to gain full understanding of such passages of Scripture and also the position that is now open to the believer in The New Covenant. It would be my understanding of The New Covenant, in order to gain most from the Giving of the Terms Section, to study both the teaching of Jesus and also the interpretation of the Apostles that we have on Scriptural record.

In His teaching, Jesus clearly taught that there was going to be a new status and experience and interaction with The Holy Spirit. In John 7:37-39, *"On the last day, that great day of the feast, Jesus* stood *and cried out saying, 'If anyone thirsts, let him come to Me and drink. He who believes in Me, as the Scripture has said, out of his heart will flow rivers of living water.'"* Jesus is teaching that those who come to Him will be able to drink and be satisfied with the rivers of Living Water that would shortly be available through the coming of The Holy Spirit. In Chapters 14 and 15, of that same Gospel, Jesus expands on the relationship between Himself, The Father and The Holy Spirit Who would be shed abroad in all the earth in the fairly near future, and indeed, this prophecy was fulfilled on the Day of Pentecost as recorded in Acts 2 and linked to the prophecy of Joel in the Old Testament.

Step 8—Eat a Memorial Meal

From our discussion so far, and comments made under this Step in a previous chapter, the roots of this covenant meal go back to Genesis 14 where we saw Melchizedek appearing out of apparently nowhere and bringing out bread and wine when blessing Abram, as priest of God Most High. The significance of these covenant elements appear prior to the main ceremony recorded in Genesis 15 and, as every Jew would know, they spoke of a covenant feast full of symbolism where the individuals of the covenant were identifying themselves with the slaughter of the animals whose blood had been shed and that these were substitutionary symbols of the real thing so that the parties coming into covenant would be free to live their lives in the shadow of the arrangement into which they had just entered.

The record we referred to in Luke 22:17-20, is a record of Jesus taking this covenant meal from the Blood Covenant Ceremony and ordaining it into a Memorial Ceremony whereby He personally was to be remembered and the tremendous significance of the final Blood Sacrifice sufficient for ALL time and eternity that He would make in the very near future, and ordaining this ancient element of Blood Covenant Ceremony as a main link of worth and significance in The New Covenant. "*Then He took the cup, and gave thanks, and said, 'Take this and divide it among yourselves, for I say to you I will not drink of the fruit of the vine until the kingdom of God comes.' And He took the bread, gave thanks and brake it, and gave it to them, saying, 'This is My body which is given for you; do this in remembrance of Me.' Likewise He also took the cup after supper, saying, 'This cup is the new covenant in My blood, which is shed for you.'*"

Major differences in theological stance arise out of the understanding and practice of a Christian Communion, Eucharist, Mass, the Lord's Supper, or other title given to this ceremony or similar ceremonies in our society today. It is my opinion, that due to the lack of understanding of the Blood Covenant Ceremony, its substitutionary symbolism, and our various attempts to be in obedience to the Lord's command, there is a variance across Christendom in the understanding and practice regarding today's use of this memorial meal. This step, out of all the individual steps of the Blood Covenant, remains the closest to the original and its worth and meaning should not be overstated nor diminished.

Step 9—Plant a Tree

Whilst this final step in The New Covenant may appear to be somewhat repetitious of Step 6, the Apostles referred to the Cross as speaking of a symbol of the work of Calvary. I suppose that if all the pieces of wood claiming to be part of the Cross of Jesus Christ the world over were to be put together, we would end up with a mighty forest, which no doubt in today's world, would rapidly be put under conservation. However, we should note that the Apostle Peter in 1 Peter 2:24, refers to a tree as that which bore the Body of Christ. It can be seen that the tree on which Jesus was crucified has become a permanent witness to the world of His Commission, His obedience and His message of glorious Salvation for those who will believe in the complete work that He has done "…*who Himself bore our sins in His own body on the tree, that* we, *having died to sins, might live for righteousness—by whose stripes you were healed."*

BIBLICAL BLOOD COVENANT CEREMONY

THE STEP	SIGNIFICANCE	REFERENCE
Exchange of Coats	Person/Life	1 Sam. 18:4a
Exchange of Belts	Belt held weapons	1 Sam. 18:4b
Cut Covenant & Covenant Walk	Innocent animals blood shed— identify united Parties	Gen 15:9, 10, 17-21. Amos 3:3
Striking hands & mingling bloods	Excange of life— see "Scar"	Lev. 17:11,14
Exchange of Names	Nature/Character exchange	Gen. 17:2-5, 15
Make a Scar	A Permanent Testifier	Isa. 49:16 John 20:24-29
Give Terms	Exchange Assets & Liabilities, Blessings & Curses	Gen. 15: 18-20, 17:6-8
Eat a Memorial Meal	Bread & Wine used as Symbols of flesh & blood	Gen. 14:18 Luke 22:24-29
Plant a Tree	A Permanent Witness to ALL	Gen. 21:32,33

LINKS BETWEEN BLOOD COVENANT CEREMONY AND THE NEW COVENANT AND GOD'S PLAN OF SALVATION FOR ALL MANKIND

THE STEP	REPRESENTING	SALVATION PLAN LINK
Exchange Coats 1 Sam. 18.4	Person/Life	Spiritual Bath John 3:6,7
Exchange Belts 1 Sam 18:4	My Weapons/Might at Your Disposal	God's Spiritual Armoury—ours. Eph. 6:10-18 Jn. 16:23,24
Cut the Covenant Gen. 15:10	Innocent animal blood shed— Covenant Walk	God's Lamb slain 1 Cor. 5:7,8 1 Pt. 1:18, 19
Striking hands cf Ruth 4:7,8	Intermingling of Blood—Mixing of lives	Jesus Deity/Humanity Jn. 1:9-13 Jn.19:34-37. Heb. 10: 3-7 Lk. 24:36-40
Exchange of Names Gen. 17:5, 15 1 Pt. 4:16	Name/Character exchange	"Christian"—Christ's man. Fruit of the Spirit. Gal. 5:16, 17, 22.
Make a scar Gen. 17:11	A Permanent Testifier Isa. 49:16	The Cross Jn. 20:27
Give Terms Gen. 17: 5-8	Exchange assets & liabilities	His Assets for my liabilities 2 Cor. 8,9 Eph. 2:4-7
Eat a Memorial Meal Gen. 14:18 1 Cor.11:23-26	Bread & Wine used as Symbols	Identical—The Lord's Supper Lk. 22:17-22
Plant a Tree Gen. 21:23	A Permanent Testifier to ALL	The Cross—God's Tree 1 Pt. 2:24 1 Cor. 1:17, 18

Questions on Chapter 5

Due to the centrality of the Christian Message covered by the material in this chapter, it is obvious that we cannot contain questions on the chapter to ten.

1. As the Exchange of Coats symbolised life and person exchange in the ceremony, (a) what key difference is involved in The New Covenant which is only possible by the work of Jesus and The Holy Spirit? (b) What term was used for the new state of the spirit of man in The New Covenant relationship? And (c) what type of experience must the believer receive when accepting this part of The New Covenant as part of the Salvation Plan of God?

2. What are the two main pieces of weaponry symbolised in the exchange of belts that are now available to the Christian?

3. In his letter to the Ephesian Church, what is the basic weaponry thought to have been used as a model for the Christians armour?

4. Why is it that the seventh item is not likened to a soldier's weaponry'?

5. Why do you think it is futile to keep putting on these various pieces of armour on a daily basis as some have practised and still do practise?

6. In the Cutting of the Covenant (a) what does Paul liken Christ to?, (b) what is the significance of giving Christ this title?, (c) what element of Cutting of Covenant does the Apostle Peter place of far greater worth and value than silver and gold or other material things?

7. In the Exchange of Names the term "Christian" is only a logical name for the person becoming involved with The New Covenant; what is the literal meaning of this name?

8. Since in the Biblical Terms the name of a person shows their character as well as their nature, what multi-faceted characteristic should the Christian display to the world that would reveal the character and nature of Christ?

9. What amazing characteristic does a baby show that becomes a key factor in The New Covenant and the striking of hands in the Blood Covenant Ceremony?

10. What Biblical story known to so many through Christmas Plays etc. takes on new significance in the light of the concept of covenant and, in particular, The New Covenant?

11. What special purpose did the blood of Jesus have in The New Covenant and where was it ultimately spilled?

12. As the scars that appeared on the Body of Jesus were apparently for Thomas's benefit only, do you think this is true, or what other possible use will they have at some future date?

13. The giving of terms to a covenant and its promises have great significance. Make a fist of 20 blessings or benefits that you can find in the Scriptures given either by Jesus or the Apostles in their teaching.

14. What 3 elements were present in a Hebrew/Blood Covenant ceremony Memorial Meal, and how do these relate to the present day application of this meal?

15. Why would the participants at The Last Supper have no problem in understanding when Jesus used food from the table and ordained it to be a lasting memorial in memory of Him?

16. In planting a tree as a permanent witness to a covenant, what has become the greatest witness of all time to The New Covenant?

SECTION 2

6

SO WHAT?

In introducing this new section we now come to a place where we have to pose the question and say exactly what this chapter is headed—SO WHAT? It always amazes me, having lived much of my life as a practising engineer, how some people can be presented with the most wonderful factual information and totally fail to see how to apply such things to practical living or individual situations. If you are one of these folks please do not be offended, and I will try to work some things through with you.

Over recent times there have been winds of change, "new" thinking and practices, and other voices and doctrines that have made shipwreck of many many lives for one very simple reason. Due to lack of teaching with Bible referenced standards, many have jumped into a power vacuum that has been created because of this lack of sound Biblically based preaching and teaching, and caused many to be mightily confused and flounder around as was the case in the early church when similar things happened then. Today we are blessed by having in our hands the Bible in many translations and paraphrases so that we can compare Scripture with Scripture and work with sound hermeneutical principles in order to get a sound and balanced view on a particular issue, and this in turn begs the question—"What did people do before they had a Bible or Scriptures?" I believe that the answer to such a question is that they had a Covenant with the Living God and that the respect and dynamic of those days is something that is lacking in the western church of today. In those days people lived in a day-to-day relationship with the Living God being led by God fearing men who heard from God and led a people who respected and feared Him in reverence and awe, knowing that they could call on Him in time of need and if they would only keep the terms of that Covenant they would be kept by His miracle working power no matter how impossible a situation may seem. The great deliverance from Egypt of the Hebrew nation after years of oppression under the effects of occult gods and tyrannical slave masters is an early example at a national level. It was Covenant obligation on God's part that saved the nation out of bondage that had ensnared them for so many years; Exodus 3:7-10 explains God's obligation and desire to progress the situation after the cries of His people for so long. "*And the* Lord *said, 'I have surely seen the oppression of My people who are in Egypt, and have heard their cry because* of *their taskmasters, for I know their sorrows. So I have* come *down to deliver them out of the hand of the Egyptians, and to bring them up from that to a good and large land, to a land flowing with milk and honey, to the place of the Canaanites and the Hittites and the Amorites and the Perizzites arid the Hivites and the Jebusites. Now therefore, behold, the cry of the children of Israel has come to Me, and I have also seen the oppression with which the Egyptians oppress them. Come now, therefore, and I will send you to Pharaoh that you may bring My people, the children of Israel, out of Egypt.'*" Prayer always plays a major role prior to a sovereign move of God at any level.

We know that the Covenant that applied in the above case has been superseded by the "New Covenant" that Jesus has brought to us and is of greater power and effect than that which operated in the Old Testament.

At this point it may be worthwhile expanding out our understanding of Covenant and looking more closely at the roots in order to see what is involved in such things as obligations, the powers with which we are getting involved and the consequences of failing to meet these obligations. The first point to be made is that we must be reminded that we are dealing with concepts that are ancient and therefore to our western sophisticated developed mindset we are already considered to be "old fashioned", "out of date", 'Irrelevant", "out of our tree", etc., etc. My reply to such comment is—"So What?!!"—my point is that our western mindset has dismissed and rejected the significance and benefit of Covenant even before we begin; so hold on and listen up because we might just learn something instead of "throwing the baby out with the bath water!"

The next point to observe is that there is a definite spiritual element involved which is much more than some commercial contract, or legal document. From Section 1 you will remember that in both the Heathenistic and Hebrew/Biblical ceremony a priest or holy man of some kind was always present and involved. If not, then the ceremony was considered to be in the presence of God as a silent witness, as with David and Jonathan. In the early Semitic period, a type of covenant existed among Arabs in order to bring about a "blood brotherhood". In this case the parties drank each other's blood in the ceremony, and it usually meant that one had been adopted into the tribe or clan of the other. A further aspect of this Covenant was that each placed themselves under the control of the other party's god, as it was considered that the god was kindred to the clan, and therefore protected the kindred blood taken by the stranger. It is because of this aspect of such covenants that the Hebrews were strictly forbidden to intermarry with foreigners or have anything to do with their gods. Jehovah had expressed Himself a jealous God on this issue, and the Old Testament carries many stories of Israel's "adulterous" relationships, and the dire consequences of their actions. Thus from the start there is an element that we today find hard to acknowledge and understand with our natural thinking; hence we need to come to the "New Covenant" and enter it by FAITH in the work that has been done on our behalf by Jesus in fulfilling the Godly Commission given to Him by the Father. This is a great leveller, as it means that no matter how good we think we are or ever could be, we can never better the perfect work that not only has been done by Jesus, but ratified by the Father and confirmed to all generations by raising Jesus from the dead by the power of the Holy Spirit. Paul confirmed this in his address at the Areopagus—Acts 17; 30,31: *"Truly, these times* of *ignorance* God *overlooked, but now commands all men everywhere to repent, because He has appointed a day on which He will judge the world in righteousness by the Man whom He has ordained. He has given assurance of this* to *all by raising Him from the dead."* When we do acknowledge the work that Jesus has done on our behalf, then we MUST accept His terms of this "New Covenant" if we are to expect the protective aspects that are to be had from this fantastic relationship between God and man.

I believe that here is the basic reason why the Church today in the continents of Africa and South America, and many other places where a simple people have placed a simple faith in a great God. have seen many many miracles and displays of God's Power that we in our sophisticated society will not see until we come to a place of humility instead of pride, and a place of submission to God's ways instead of our own ways. In Britain today it is these aspects that we have neglected to our peril, and no matter how "politically incorrect" it may be considered to be, I believe that until we address these matters and return to Christian Godly values and ways we will continue to slide down an evermore slippery slope in national and international happenings. By our name—BRITISH—we are by interpretation of that name *Brit*—"Covenant"—from Hebrew *beryth* meaning league or covenant and passing between pieces (Strongs 1285 & 1262). *Ish*—"man/people"—from Hebrew *iysh* meaning man or people, (Strongs 0376) i.e. people of Covenant. We desperately need leaders who both understand these aspects and dare to correct them at a national and international level. Such leadership needs to appear in both Church and State "corridors of power". I believe it is going to take a move of Almighty God to bring such about. Be not dismayed, He did it for His people in Egypt, and we are in a greater Covenant relationship with Him in the "New Covenant" now than then. If His Sovereign Hand were to move on our land now, how much more responsibility would that place on us to fulfil Covenant Terms relative to this "New Covenant".

As we continue to ask these simple questions, and as we begin to appreciate what we have in our hands, it should readily be apparent that here is something which although we may not have fully understood when we first came into Covenant, we must now do something about finding out more of that which we now say we are part of, and also realize that this is a very serious matter, that it is an everlasting Covenant into which we have come, and not just some 'please yourself, will I, won't I bother' to play some game of church politics, but that here is the essence of eternal life through Jesus Christ—and if we are not serious about it, He certainly is!

In the remaining chapters of this Section I will attempt to put to you what I believe are the effects of Covenant that reach down to a very deep personal level. That is my "So What?" reply to the effects of Covenant on the individual, a group, or Society

Questions on Chapter 6

1. What is the author's suggested reason why many today have made shipwreck of their lives?

2. What is the suggested basic foundation that people had prior to Biblical scriptures?

3. In those ancient days what characteristic was displayed that is lacking in modern Society?

4. What obligation did these people feel necessary to have in their lives to expect Godly involvement for themselves?

5. What is the significance of spiritual aspects of Covenant for the Hebrew nation?

6. Why were the Jews forbidden to intermarry with other people of heathen nations?

7. What do you understand would he the dire consequences of Covenant breaking at a tribal or national level?

8. Do you see any significant links to modern Society in western nations in the foregoing questions?

9. In a parallel scenario, why do you think the Church is so weak in Britain or other western society nations today, whilst other nations in other parts of the world are so much more strong and dynamic?

10. What steps do you think are necessary to correct Covenant breaking in a person, group, clan or tribe, or nation no matter where they may be located geographically?

7

WHO AM I?

In these next chapters I will attempt to show the significance of the New Covenant that is ours in Christ in answering some fundamental questions. The first of these is **Who am I?**

In the days of the Covenanters in the troubled times of the 1600's era in Scotland there were those who signed a covenant to stand against political and religious persecution. Some signed in their own blood after having first made a cut in their arm and filling the pen with their life blood. This resulted in them banding together to stand for Biblical values against the Establishment who viewed them as rebels, and resulted in perilous times. During this era many committed their lives to Jesus Christ as Lord and Saviour and having responded to the challenge of the message of the Gospel gave their lives and loyalty to Jesus as Head of their lives and of His Church. During these times the new convert was taken to a godly minister to "enter the Covenant". As to what exactly took place in this encounter is uncertain, but I believe it would be spending time with the minister and being taught the fundamentals of the Christian Faith with a particular bias of the relevance and life encounter with God in Christ Jesus and the New Covenant that He has brought to mankind. It is this kind of teaching that kept the Covenanters through horrendous days of peril and gave Scotland the great Protestant heritage down subsequent generations. During those times the characteristics of those Covenanters was that they certainly knew who they were and Whose they were! It is recorded that the following is a snippet of conversation at the time of the signing of this Covenant on the 28th February 1638: "Turning to Warriston, Rev. Henderson exclaimed almost with a reverent awe, 'Lo, Archibald, how many are subscribing it with their very own blood as they draw and use it in place of ink. Truly they are pouring their own souls into this. See, some write after their signature "Until Death!" They offer their gear, their bodies and their lives as a living sacrifice, and regard it as their reasonable service…'"

Let us now consider some of these aspects. Firstly the knowledge and concept of being in a Blood Covenant relationship with the living God through Jesus Christ must have a most sobering effect on the individual. To comprehend that the Almighty God who created all things and sent the Son of the Triune Godhead from the heavenlies to become flesh and blood and be the Sacrifice of the New Covenant which would restore fellowship back to the original level of the first encounter between a Creator God and mankind at the time of creation, and much more, in that through the promises of this New Covenant an everlasting relationship of Friendship with the Living God has been established in absolute certainty and establishment in both the heavens and the earth, and is enduring past time and for ever in eternity, would certainly need explanation to both simple and educated folks in all ranks of Society both then and now.

If you have just read this last paragraph and you are uncertain of its scope and effect, please read it over several times until you can comprehend the vastness of the breadth and effect of what is both said and implied by that paragraph. Pray for understanding and wisdom of the Holy Spirit to grasp it; for here is a nugget of gold that will change you for ever once you grasp its meaning and implication,

When the writer to the Hebrews penned the words of Chapter 6 he used the phrase of "going on to maturity", and subsequently discusses the issue of Covenant. In other words, understanding Covenant is for those who are spiritually mature and beyond the simple "doctrines of Christ" that the convert is expected to know as he moves from convert to disciple. This can be interpreted as moving on from agreeing with the Gospel and changing your stance towards God and accepting the teaching of the Teacher and changing your life style to come in line with the Teacher's teaching. Here is surely a Call from heaven to "be renewed in our minds" as Paul taught, and live by faith in the work and power that the work of Calvary has brought into being. The concept of leading a disciplined life, looking to Jesus as our example and forerunner in the heavenlies, contrasts sharply with ideas that were encountered in the early Church as it grew, and also many ideas that are abroad today in Christendom. The interesting facts are that many things abroad today are just modem versions of the same old gags that tried to destroy the early Church and the apostles had to correct by their writings which we now have as our New Testament.

So what are some of the other things that I need to know in answering the question "Who am I?". To answer these important mattes, we must turn to prophetic Scriptures and see how these things have been fulfilled and are applied in the

New Covenant. We do this in order to apply the principle that when God is going to do something He first tells the prophets—Amos 3:7,8: *"Surely the Lord God does nothing, unless He reveals His secret to His servants the prophets. A lion has roared! Who will not fear! The Lord God has spoken! Who can but prophesy?"* In Jeremiah 31: 27-37 we have a major prophecy concerning the type of arrangement that the New Covenant would provide. Read this passage now for yourself and write a note of the things you would expect to see in such a new arrangement. Does your list agree with me that there will be the following: 1. There will be a united nation of Israel with Almighty God watching over them. 2. There will no longer be among God's people the consequences of sin passing down families, and generations. 3. There will be an open access for every individual directly to the living God. Everyone will "know the Lord". 4. The law of the Living God will be written on our hearts. 5. There will be a new type of forgiveness; that is, our sins will be eternally eradicated. Note that verses 35 to 37 are the terms of the Covenant that are applied to these Promises.

Let us now consider these points.

1.   In 1948 Israel appeared on the map again as a Nation. It was "birthed in a day"! God has certainly protected His people the Jews as others have tried to annihilate them for over half a century.

2.   Much in certain quarters of the Church has gone into excess, I believe, but there is power in the Name of Jesus to cleanse and break generational curses in God's people, especially for those who have become Christians and brought their spiritual "baggage" with them. This is especially true for those who have entered secret societies by oaths and binding ceremonies opening up themselves and their families to curses unto death and similar. e.g. Free Masons, Knights of St Columba, and similar.

3.   There is now open a direct way to the throne room of the living God as we pray as Jesus taught. To the Father, in Jesus' name; no need to involve a blood sacrifice—Jesus has ended the need—no need to involve a priest or other human being—the veil to the holy of holies was torn open from the top to the bottom giving open access to the Presence of the Living God. When we are in this Covenant we "know the Lord" and can enjoy the near Presence of the Lord for ourselves; thus we can commune with our God in this new and living way. We can know for ourselves what the Lord would have us do and be, for and in Him. No man in whatever guise or rank in the

Church has authority over us to tell us what God is saying in our lives. From this flows the doctrine of The Priesthood of All Believers. This should not be confused with those godly ministers in authority of the godly order of Church government. The basis of the Protestant movement and the Reformation has much to say on this matter.

4. I believe this is a direct reference to the work of the Holy Spirit who is now shed abroad in the world after Pentecost. His work is to "convict the world of sin", to be a Guide and Comforter to the believer, to prompt and clarify to us godly options in times of decision. To me all these speak of the law of God being "written on our hearts". For the believers the working and manifestations of the fruit and gifts of the Holy Spirit is a major aspect of the New Covenant and those who enter it.

5. This aspect needs to be understood by many in the Church. The effect of the work of Calvary is very far reaching and is a perfect work for both time and eternity; this is why Jesus said as He breathed his last breath, "It is finished." The finished work of Calvary both atones and sanctifies the sinner who comes to Christ and accepts the work He has done on his behalf as a perfect and finished work for all time and eternity. We can never do any good works or add to that which is a perfect finished work in order to gain our sanctification; otherwise Calvary is not a finished work. In my opinion, there is confusion in some parts of the Church over this matter, and leads to false doctrine and burdensome practice to achieve what is already perfected and accepted by the Father, the proof of which is, that Jesus is risen from the dead, ascended into the heavenlies, sits at the Father's right hand and is interceding the New Covenant for us.

When we consider these aspects of the New Covenant which are just a minimum reflection on that prophesied by Jeremiah, we must surety realize how the promises made by the prophets have come to pass. For some aspects they have come into being as Jesus brought in the New Covenant or shortly afterwards, and for other aspects it has taken hundreds of years, but for we who live in these days there is blessing and benefit to be had with confirmation of these things still being fulfilled even in our lifetime in a literal way. As we looked at the items of Ceremony in the Covenant and the resultant effect, we also can enter into such a realization and claim our rightful position that we now have "in Christ". This may seem almost too obvious, but it is the exercising of our Covenant position in this New Covenant that is going to make all the difference. What is that position?

If you remember, the resultant relationship at the end of the Covenant Ceremony was that the parties were "Friends". In our western society this is usually considered to be a casual acquaintance. If there is anything more we add other words to expand out the meaning such as "Special Friend", "Best Friend", "Lifelong Friend" and so forth, but a Covenant Friend is ALL of these and much more. A Covenant Friend is one who would die for us—literally; a Covenant Friend will defend us at all levels, and on all occasions when we ask him to and in our absence will defend our corner when we are not there. There is solid support and devotion because of the commitment of Covenant that is assumed by both parties each to the other.

I wonder how many of us understand that Jesus has committed Himself to us at that level when we become Christian because we have entered Covenant with Him and He has entered into Covenant with us when He came and brought in the New Covenant which was the plan of the Father, effected into being by the Son, and is still in effect today by the working of the Holy Spirit who is alive and effective in the whole earth today and until Jesus comes again. So the more we understand the status of a Friend we will then begin to understand "Who I am". Jesus spoke plainly to His disciples on this matter in John15:12-17: *"This is My commandment, that you love one another as I have loved you. Greater love has no man than this, than to lay down one's life for his friends. You are My friends if you do whatever I command you. No longer do I call you servants, for a servant does not know what his master is doing; but I have called you friends, for all things that I heard from My Father I have made known to you. You did not choose Me, but I chose you and appointed you that you should go and bear fruit, and that your fruit should remain, that whatever you ask the Father in My name He may give you. These things I command you, that you love one another."* Here Jesus is making the distinction between servants and friends as the title with which He addresses them, and goes on to say that servants do not know what the master is doing, but friends do. Here is a clear teaching of the relationship that those in Covenant have between themselves and the Father through Jesus in the New Covenant. This is the relationship that WE have as Christians! We are party to the inner working at the heavenly throne roam because we are "in Christ" as Paul continually reminded his readers in the epistle to the Ephesians. In this passage in John's gospel, Jesus says several very important things also. He speaks of commanding us to "love one another", and goes on to say that the greatest display of this love is if we were to lay down our lives for our "Friends". It should be pointed out that we are only "Friends" if we are in Covenant together, i.e. if we are Christians, members of

HIS Church. This is the relationship we should have one to another as a normal relationship and should not squabble and fight as we do in most parts of the Church. No wonder Covenant is so little known or taught in the Church in the western society! Here are the real Covenant terms of the New Covenant! These have a bite on us that we just do not want to know because they reach to the core of our being in demanding real change in our life style that would revolutionize both society and the Church—no wonder they said of the early Church members that they turned the world upside down! If the western Church would dare to do the same today it would suffer the same criticism as those in the early Church, but what a difference our society would know!

So as a "Friend" we have both a great open relationship and a great responsibility to fulfil. Here is the basis of a fantastic standing which challenges our whole person to be radical, daring, and different, instead of being slushed along by the tide of moral decay, cant and humbug that is in Society today, or squeezed into the mould of the New World Order with its assertive authoritarianism and sinister secular tentacles which is attempting to rub out the inheritance of generations as well as freedom of expression. No wonder the Scottish Covenanters of old stood against the tide of unbiblical standards that were imposed in their day to leave us a bright light of example and encouragement if only we too will find the strength of true "Friendship".

Questions on Chapter 7

1. In attempting to answer the question "Who am I?" what has been the basis of founding our search to such a question?

2. In making comparison to a time in previous history, what time frame and people were used as our example to consider?

3. Although this group was involved with the contentious politics of their day, on what was the dual basis of their strength firmly planted?

4. From our studies in section 1, what relationship do we consider is worth further attention to our researches as a basis of finding a solid foundation on which to build our lives in times of adversity?

5. From the Old Testament Scriptures, on what basis can we be assured that the work that Jesus did was planned from the heavens and not just a disastrous event of history?

6. Why can we take notice of the prophetic message of Jeremiah considered in this chapter—two aspects should be evident?

7. If "Friendship" is the resultant relationship of Covenant, why can the Christian be so confident in this relationship whilst here in this life on earth?

8. Further to 7, what element of becoming a Christian confounds many religious people in the Church, and sets those who have this understanding apart from Society and secular and natural thinking?

9. What place does the Holy Spirit play in (a) the confirming work of acceptance by God of the work Jesus did in bringing the New Covenant, and (b) the daily living of Christians the world over?

10. If the answer to "who am I?" is that I am the Friend of the Living God because I have entered the New Covenant that Jesus brought, what sort of a person does that make me in this world?

8

WHAT DO I HAVE?

Having discovered at least the main aspect of "who I am" we now turn to answering the aspect of the question "So What?" by asking another question which is "What do I have in this relationship of Friendship?"—we are of course referring to that Friendship which is in the New Covenant.

Once we have understood this relationship and it has not only dawned on our minds who we are, but also in our spirit,—our innermost man—has understood this, then we can begin to grasp the great provision that is in our salvation package purchased at such great cost at Calvary by Jesus.

We must also very quickly change our thinking once we realize "Who we ARE". This change alone is a major transformation in our mindset, and we must renew our minds as the Apostle Paul encourages us to do in Romans 12:2: "*And do not be conformed to this world, but be transformed by the renewing of your mind, that you may prove what is that good and acceptable and perfect will of God.*" And Colossians 3:2: "*Set your mind on things above, not on things on the earth.*" This I believe is the process of "understanding" and is a work of the Holy Spirit and a manifestation of His gifting in the life of the Christian. It is a spiritual work by the Spirit of God, it is an applied work of revelation and wisdom that only the Holy Spirit can do, and it is His ordained working in our lives to equip us for the prepared works that He has called us to do in working out our salvation whilst here on this earth. It is only when we can accept in our minds "WHO we are" that it will make any sense in understanding not only WHAT we have been given, but WHY we have been given it. We need to change our thinking so that we become "spiritually" minded beings who have this position "in Christ" and not continue in our "natural" or former ways of thinking. If we fail to be in balance on this issue we will fall into one of two ways of behaviour; either become "religious" or go "super-spiritual", both of which display a pattern that I believe is not of the Spirit of God, but sadly is much in evidence in the Church today.

As we grow in maturity as "spiritual" men and women we will quickly appreciate that our natural or sexual status has absolutely nothing to do with our position "in Christ" or our Covenant standing "in Him".

It has taken the Church years and generations to get its head round this and indeed it is in its head that the problem lies. For if we do not understand our salvation, that we are born again of the Spirit of God, that we get this new birth by a spiritual process which is a divine interaction with the Holy Spirit and our spirit in regeneration, then we will remain "natural" men and women instead of becoming "sons" of the Living God in Covenant with Him. We also need to understand that we were not born "from above" to continue a natural existence for eternity, but that our new life in Covenant "in Christ" imparts to us the divine nature which is eternal and has no need for the gender aspects which are confined to the need to procreate human life to continue our existence in this natural world only. Therefore, if we have a difficulty in the manifestation of anointed ministries that are more than apparent in women and we think this should not be so, then my answer is twofold. Firstly, refer the matter in prayer to our Creator God who created such a person with the spiritual anointing, and secondly be mature enough to recognize that the Scriptures teach that it is a spiritual work of the Holy Spirit to enable the manifestations of the ninefold gifts among the believers, and Christ as Head of the Church gives the fivefold ascension gift ministries for the maturing of the saints as proclaimed by the Apostle in 1 Corinthians 12 and Ephesians 4. In other words these are heavenly works for us to appreciate and praise our heavenly Father for, and we should not gripe because we do not see things His way!

So back to the question of "What do I have?" The main thing to be appreciated is our new position in Covenant with Christ. We need to understand the concept that our God has entered into with us in Blood Covenant, that is a total commitment to each other in an eternal unbreakable bond for eternity. The oath of the Covenant has been sworn by the One of whom there is none higher nor ever will be for ever; therefore we have entered into a position "in Christ" that is unassailable by any other spiritual power or force in all the earth or the heavens and any other place also. If we can understand this, then the other gifts and weapons and anything else that we have access to "in Christ", become mighty tools in our hands in both the natural realm and the spiritual also.

Having said all that, there is something else that we should understand very quickly once we have become Christians and begin to realize "Who we are, and

Whose we are" and that this Christian life that we have entered into is not a picnic but an outright war that is in a spiritual realm, and now that we have been "born again by the Spirit of God", we have become alive to a world that we never really knew much about because we were only alive in the natural world. We now know that Man, male and female, actually lives in two worlds, a natural world and also a spirit world. Before this new birth and regeneration, in our natural state we knew nothing of this spirit world because we were in a fallen or sinful state controlled by Satan and his host of followers in that spirit world and were dead towards God! But now being alive towards God in this new world we become a threat towards Satan whom Jesus defeated at Calvary and he still wars against the saints or followers of Jesus Christ today. You may say that this is all a new idea, and you have never heard of this sort of thing before. I am not here to doubt you, but because you may not have heard this before tells me that sadly you are probably in a state that many are placed in today's Church. One of the greatest war strategies that an enemy can effect is to convince his opposition that he does not exist. Simple, isn't it! No problem—NO problem! This is one of Satan's great strategies that is effective in the Church. If you do not believe he exists you will not disturb him or oppose him, so in one swipe he has silenced you. How did he bring this about? He planted an idea, a false idea, or a lie, and you believed the lie and decided that Satan was not worth bothering about. You were deceived just like Eve in the creation story in Genesis. Tell me, how did you come to such a conclusion? You may say, "I don't know, I just decided." Friend, you just blew it—we are now "in Christ" and have God's spiritual weaponry at our disposal so that we can defeat Satan just like Jesus did, because we are in Covenant and we are "in Christ". Where do I get that from? It is simple—its Covenant! Look back at Section 1, pages 38-39 (tables). HIS weapons at MY disposal. So what weaponry did I not use that I could have done? In Revelation 12:10,11 we read, "*Then I heard a loud voice saying in heaven, 'Now salvation, and strength, and the kingdom of our God, and the power of His Christ have come, for the accuser of our brethren, who accused them before our God day and night, has been cast down.' And they overcame him by the blood of the Lamb and by the word of their testimony, and they did not love their lives to the death.*" Here we have a prophetic confirmation of the teaching that Jesus gave in John 14:11-14: "*Believe Me that I am in the Father and the Father in Me, or else believe Me for the sake of the works themselves. Most assuredly, I say to you, he who believes in Me, the works that I do he will do also: and greater works than these he will do, because I go to My Father.*" This is the core of the New Covenant, i.e. prayer in the NAME of Jesus, and with it the boldness to tell forth the truth of the Gospel, i.e. testimony, and the BLOOD of Jesus.

Also in the Revelation passage please note the level of commitment "unto death", i.e. TOTAL commitment to Jesus. This is not religious fervour but keeping of Covenant terms! This is the position the Scottish Covenanters and many more like them in both present and past times in many countries of the world came to realize as they knew and practised the truth of Covenant.

Are we now beginning to understand that we have moved on from our normal natural thinking and posturing to a totally new approach—that of the "spiritual" man? As we choose to allow our minds to be renewed by the invited working of the Holy Spirit within us, that is, we by prayer in Jesus Name ask and plead for His working in our lives to be effective in changing us "from glory to glory" as Paul told the Corinthian church, and we take a conscious deliberate choice to allow the Holy Spirit to change our way of thinking and therefore our practice and lifestyle as we work through the changed mindset that is now set on the things of God and not on our former lifestyle and ways. By now I am sure that you will have realized that this new lifestyle is not for wimps! By this changed lifestyle we are now exhibiting responsibility for our actions and we are now making conscious and deliberate decisions that will be effective in our lives and affecting others also. We have moved from being re-active to pro-active. We are exercising our God-given choice of free will and are not being pushed around by Satan and his ilk. We are therefore in a continual warfare situation that is spiritual.

Our minds are the battlefield and we need Spiritual weaponry to overcome the enemy of our soul; that is why we need to be in Covenant and have access to the spiritual armoury that God gives us "in Christ" in the New Covenant.

Before we move on to expand on the weaponry that we have been given access to we must first clear up the point made previously that you had blown it when you took the decision yourself. If we do fall to temptation, there is a perfect provision in our God in this New Covenant. In 1 John 1:5-10 we read, *"This is the message we have heard from Him and declare to you, that God is light and in Him is no darkness at all. If we say that we have fellowship with Him, and walk in darkness, we lie and do not practice the truth. But if we walk in the light as He is in the light, we have fellowship with one another, and the blood of Jesus Christ His Son cleanses us from all sin. If we say that we have no sin, we deceive ourselves, and the truth is not in us. If we confess our sins, He is faithful and just to forgive us our sins and to cleanse us from all unrighteousness. If we say that we have not sinned we make Him a liar, and His word is not in us."* John is teaching a great truth that is based on the New

Covenant. He speaks of fellowship with God and one another, and the basis of that is "the blood of Jesus"—our New Covenant relationship—as a means of cleansing us from "all" sin when we confess our sin to Him. He is both faithful and just and WILL forgive our sins. So what happens when we are tempted to sin? It isn't sin to be tempted; it becomes sin when we yield to the temptation. Sometimes we make a deliberate decision knowing full well the consequences of our decision and choose to sin, but other times we are deceived by Satan into believing that we are making a good decision when actually our pride blinds us and our natural decision making is no match for the spiritual aspects of the temptation and therefore we fall into sin. This is the story at creation time and how Man, male and female, fell from open fellowship with God on a one-to-one basis. Because we can be cleansed by the Blood of Jesus we can have that open fellowship restored and in our daily lives know that open relationship with our God once again through the working out of the New Covenant in our lives.

So the things we have seen in this chapter so far that we have been given the use of are (1) our standing in our God now that we are in Covenant with Him, (2) the use of the Name of Jesus in powerful prayer, and (3) the Blood of Jesus as the powerful parts of the New Covenant weaponry. To do justice on the fuller aspects of this provision will need to be a separate work in another book, but before we close this chapter there is another list of weaponry that has in recent years become the focus of some teaching which can become lopsided and burdensome in its application, and I would like to address that before we move on.

In Ephesians 6:10-20 Paul is writing to the Ephesian Church and it is thought that at the time of writing he was either chained to or within regular sight of a Roman soldier. In this passage he speaks of the "amour of God' and proceeds to list out the various parts that would correspond to a Roman soldier's battle dress, and make comparison to the spiritual weaponry that is ours "in Christ" and in the New Covenant. The parts of the armoury being compared I believe speak for themselves, but I must make observation on the application that many have made of this passage in an attempt to bring some balance in application. *"Finally, my brethren, be strong in the Lord and in the power of His might. Put on the whole armour of God, that you may be able to stand against the wiles of the devil. For we do not wrestle against flesh and blood, but against principalities, against powers, against the rulers of the darkness of this age, against spiritual hosts of wickedness in the heavenly places. Therefore take up the whole armour of God, that you may be able to withstand in the evil day, and having done all, to stand. Stand therefore, having girded your waist with truth, having put on the breastplate of righteousness, and having shod your feet with the preparation of the gospel of peace; above all, taking the shield of faith with which you will be able to quench all the fiery darts of the wicked one. And take the helmet of salvation, and the sword of the Spirit, which is the word of God; praying always with all prayer and supplication in the Spirit, being watchful to this end with all perseverance and supplication for all the saints."*

Firstly, observe verse 12, where the type of weaponry is clearly identified. It is spiritual and NOT natural. It is dealing with principalities, powers, world rulers, and spiritual hosts of wickedness in the heavenlies. This clearly defines the battle areas and types of foe. It also tells us where these things are NOT, so we must hold a balanced view of these matters in order to avoid going into extremes and excess.

Next, note that Paul NEVER talks of taking it off!! This is a status that we HAVE in the New Covenant provision, and as we do not have to get saved every day, but enter a standing in our God "in Christ", so also we must never try to take off our armour because we are always in the battle with Satan and his host and do NOT rely on our own strength as this is only pride on our part. Some have entered into a practice of "putting on the armour" as a daily religious ritual prior to leaving the house every day. My question to those who practice this ritual is—when did you ever take the armour off?

Do you think that God's provision is suddenly ineffective overnight, or if the going gets a bit tough, or some other reason? Friend, this is a battle for 24 hours a day and 365 days a year and from eternity until Jesus comes and we are in His nearer presence in the heavenlies with Him. We dare not even contemplate taking off God's provision, so see this for what it is—a Satanic deception, to make you think you are vulnerable for some part of the time or that God's provision is somehow only on part-time coverage and is up to you to make some alternative provision. Jesus did a perfect work and as such God accepted it! Do not let Satan deceive you into believing it is anything else.

Lastly, with regard to the armour described in this passage, have a count at the number of pieces that you think it has! Now count again to make sure that you are sure that you have all of them. How many can you see? Most can only see SIX, but for the mature they see SEVEN, the number of perfection. Most people just count the bits and pieces of the Roman battle dress and stop with the sword. This totals SIX which is the number of Man. If we stop here we have a religious provision that ends up in ritual, but if we take note of the GREAT spiritual model and see the seventh weapon,—PRAYER IN THE SPIRIT AT ALL TIMES—we reveal the secret weaponry of God! What is this "prayer in the Spirit?" I believe it is one of the assets given to the spiritual man, praying in the language of the Holy Spirit, or praying in tongues. No wonder Satan does not want you to know about this weapon! Religious people make it controversial as an excuse to steer clear; others make mockery about it and do Satan's work for him; but for the spiritual man of maturity it is a mighty weapon of great effectiveness that Satan has no power over, since, I believe, we are praying directly into the heavenlies as the Holy Spirit leads us. Paul spoke of this and the levels of intensity in his letter to the Romans 8: 26,27: *"Likewise the Spirit also helps us in our weaknesses. For we do not know what we should pray for as we ought, but the Spirit Himself makes intercession for us with groanings that cannot be uttered. Now He who searches the hearts knows what the mind of the Spirit is, because He makes intercession for the saints according to the will of God."* Here again, we have the work of the Comforter, the Holy Spirit helping us in prayer. So in summary of "what we have" in the New Covenant, I have touched on a very short list of provisions, but there is much more and these will need to be addressed another time. If we can mature to the point of entering into these provisions, we will be an effective soldier of the Cross and do much damage for the gospel of Christ as we progress in maturity.

Questions on Chapter 8

1. Explain the key elements in the work of "understanding".

2. Why does entry to the New Covenant place us in an unassailable position?

3. How many worlds does Man live in, and what are they?

4. In becoming aware of our new standing and environment, what is the key factor of communication that has been restored to us, and what is its significance?

5. List the four items covered in this chapter that are available to those who have entered the New Covenant.

6. In the use of the two items that were referred to in Scripture in Revelation, what were the terms and conditions that accompanied those who used these weapons with great effect?

7. What were the characteristics that Paul identified to the Ephesians of the armoury that he then listed?

8. Explain the significance in the number of piece parts that can be identified, their comparison, numerical significance, and why the last piece is so often missed by many people?

9. Why is this last weapon thought to be so effective against Satan and his host?

10. Explain the main differences between the "natural" and the "spiritual" man.

9

WHERE AM I GOING?

I wonder how many times we have asked this question, and indeed how many people know the answer to such a question when referred to their lives? Once we have become Christians we enter a new world that we never really knew before, that opens to us so much more, and as we change our ways of living and rejoice in the new relationship that we have entered into we need to become aware of the great things that we now have open to us and learn how to handle ourselves and the new life that we have "in Christ". If we are aware of the New Covenant and what Jesus has done for us we have a great framework in which to grow as we are taught the things of God by a good teacher, learning to be a disciple of Jesus Christ and knowing the certainty of the commitment He has made to us. It must be pointed out that there is a difference between a disciple and a convert. The convert has agreed to turn from his former ways towards Christ, but a disciple is one who has allowed himself to come under the teaching of Christ, and displays a level of commitment and discipline to put into practice the teachings of Christ, his Teacher. The hard part is changing our ways and earning to be obedient to the ways of walking by faith in our new found Friend!

The main reason we find such a change to be so tough is that in these times we are living in a world that is so rebellious to our God, His ways and values, and those things that the Scriptures declare to us. We quickly find that if we are going to be faithful to the ways of the New Covenant we have great opposition not only in the ways we have discussed so far, but also from our family members, work mates, social contacts and so on. In fact, we soon discover that we have truly become different because of the new birth we have experienced, and that truly, we are under attack from all sides. We now see things from a different viewpoint, God's viewpoint, and so it happens that as we see things from this new viewpoint our desires change from the desire for the "works of the flesh" referred to in Galatians 5:19-21 (adultery, fornication, uncleanness, lewdness, idolatry, sorcery, hatred, contentions, jealousies, outbursts of wrath, selfish ambitions, dissensions, heresies, envy. murders, drunkenness, revelries, and the like), to letting the "fruit of the Spirit" (love, joy, peace, longsuffering, kindness, goodness, faithfulness, gentleness, self-control), manifest in our lives as Paul taught in Galatians 5:22-24. You will see that there is a very painful process referred to there—crucifixion. At the time of writing Paul used a term that was well known and explicit to those in that time of Roman dominance. If you were crucified then you certainly experienced two things: (1) a very painful process as the old life left your body, and (2) when that process was finished you were totally dead to that old life you had lived. Here Paul is trying to make the point that in our commitment to Christ in the New Covenant this sort of commitment level should be "normal". John said the same thing in Revelation 10:11 that we looked at in a previous chapter—*"And he said to me, 'You must prophesy again about many peoples, nations, tongues, and kings.'"* The issue of compromise in our daily living is something we have to work out for ourselves as we go through this life, but the great news is we are not alone—we have the Holy Spirit indwelling us and prompting us when we have to make choices, so we need to learn how to hear His voice as we travel this world. (1 Corinthians 3:16: *"Do you not know that you are the temple of God and that the Spirit of God dwells in you?"* and 2 Corinthians 6:14-18: *"Do not be unequally yoked with unbelievers. For what fellowship has righteousness with lawlessness? And what communion has light with darkness? And what accord has Christ with Belial? Or what part has a believer with an unbeliever? And what agreement has the temple of God with idols? For you are the temple of the living God. As God has said, 'I will dwell in them and walk among them. I will be their God, and they shall be My people.'"*)

To answer more directly the question this chapter poses, we must look at Ephesians 2:8-10: *"For by grace you have been saved through faith, and that not of yourselves; it is the gift of God, not of works, lest anyone should boast. For we are His workmanship, created in Christ Jesus for good works, which God prepared beforehand that we should walk in them."* Here Paul is recording for us the facts of our salvation and why we are here. In God's great plan of salvation for you and me He has prepared an individual Action Plan for our lives. The Great Creator has not only entered Covenant with us but He knows us so well that He has a special work for us to do in our lives. Do not be confused about these works. We are saved by the work of Jesus on the Cross and the coming of the New Covenant, but as we enter as an individual, so God meets us as an individual and plans our lives on an individual basis. He knows our strengths and weaknesses, our skills and talents, and desires that we should fellowship with Him on a one-to-one basis as did Adam and Eve before the Fall. For some it will mean that they continue on in their career or job of work as they have done for the last so many years. For others it may mean great change in lifestyle, company that you have kept previously, or a complete change of lifestyle for which you will need help, training, or relocation to the place of action. This plan that God has is sometimes referred to as a Calling, and no matter how much change in our natural circumstances may be involved, it is our Heavenly Calling that is the important part. When we know what God's plan for our life is, and we are sure that it is His Call, and not a fancy idea that we have dreamed up, then we can be confident that our Covenant keeping God WILL be faithful and true to His plan and Calling on our lives. We will know where we are going, we will be clear that He will provide and sustain us in the pathway of our lives. Let us consider the following Scriptures—Romans 11:29: *"For the gifts and the calling of God are irrevocable"*; 1 Thessalonians 5:24: *"He who calls you is faithful, who also will do it."* Philippians 3:13,14: *"I can do all things through Christ who strengthens me."* 2 Peter 1:3-11: *"Blessed be the God and Father of our Lord Jesus* Christ, *who according to His abundant mercy has begotten us again to a living hope through the resurrection of Jesus Christ from the dead, to an inheritance incorruptible and undefiled and that does not fade away, reserved in heaven for you, who are kept by the power of God through faith for salvation ready to be revealed in the last time. In this you greatly rejoice, though now for a little while, if need be, you have been grieved by various trials, that the genuineness of your faith, being much more precious than gold that perishes, though it be tested by fire, may be found to praise, honour and glory at the revelation of Jesus Christ."* These Scriptures do not call for us to play at Church, but to be sober minded, realistic, and disciplined soldiers of the Cross of Jesus Christ. Who said being a Christian was for the weak and wacky? Certainly not anyone who knew about the New Covenant or the truth about the work of Christ on our behalf.

We can do nothing else but praise the God of our Salvation for making such wonderful provision "in Christ" and assuring us of the great heavenly reward that is ours after we pass from this life to be with Him in eternity.

Before I close this chapter I feel I must cover this last aspect—our heavenly reward. In 1 Corinthians 15:12-19: *"Now if Christ is preached that He has been raised from the dead, how do* some *among you say that there is no resurrection of the dead? But if there is no resurrection of the dead, then Christ is not risen. And if Christ is not risen, your faith is futile; you are still in your sins! Then also those who have fallen asleep in Christ have perished. If in this life only we have hope in Christ, we are of all men most miserable."* Paul is making the case of resurrection being the key factor to our hope in Christ and the evidence that God is faithful in His promise towards us by saying that if our hope in Christ is for this life only, then we are of all men most miserable. In other words, if that is true, we have been deceived and our hope of eternal life is in vain. But in fact Christ HAS been risen from the dead and is interceding in the heavenlies the New Covenant on our behalf. Jesus clearly taught that He would return to this earth and that it was His intention to have an eternal relationship with those who believe in Him. Eternal life has always been preached and taught as the end blessing and benefit of the relationship that Jesus offers to those who believe in Him. Here are some sample Scripture references—John 3:16: *"For God so loved the world that He gave His only begotten Son, that whoever believes in Him should not perish but have everlasting life"*; John. 4:13,14: *"Jesus answered and said to her, 'Whoever drinks of this water will thirst again, but whoever drinks of the water that I shall give him will become in him a fountain of water springing up into everlasting life.'"* Luke 18:29,30: *"And He said to them, Assuredly, I say to you, there is no one who has left house, or parents or brothers or wife, or children, for the sake of the kingdom of God, who shall not receive many times more in this present time, and in the age to come eternal life."* Galatians 6:7,8: *"Do not be deceived. God is not mocked; for whatever a man sows, that he will also reap. For he who sows to his flesh will of the flesh reap corruption, but he who sows to the Spirit will of the Spirit reap everlasting life."* Romans 6:22,23: *"But now having been set free from sin, and having become slaves of God, you have your fruit to holiness, and the end, everlasting life. For the wages of sin is death, but the gift of God is eternal life in Christ Jesus our Lord."* 2 Thessalonians 2:16,17: *"Now may our Lord Jesus Christ Himself, and our God and Father, who has loved us and given us everlasting consolation and good hope by grace, comfort your hearts and establish you in every good word and work."*

Jesus taught specifically on this matter in John 14:1-7,18,19, showing that He was not a here today, gone tomorrow, and that was the end of the matter kind of Person! He said, *"Let not your heart be troubled, you believe in God, believe also in Me. In My Father's house are many mansions; if it were not so, I would have told you. I go to prepare a place for you. And if I go and prepare a place for you, I will come again and receive you to Myself; that where I am, there you may be also. And where I go you know, and the way you know."* Thomas said to Him, *"Lord, we do not know where you are going, and how can we know the way?"* Jesus said to him, *"I am the way, the truth and the life. No one comes to the Father except through Me. If you had known Me, you would have known My Father also; and from now on you know Him and have seen Him."* He promised to return, that there was a prepared place for his disciples, and that we would be with Him in the Father's presence eternally. This is no pie in the sky, food on a plate if you wait, or any other smart talk. This is a Godly promise just like that of Covenant, which we have shown to be of the highest certainty and reliability that it is possible to have. In other words, as we have placed our trust in Jesus for salvation and all the needs for this life in both worlds and have proved for ourselves the reality of the New Covenant promises and resources, so also we can dare to trust Jesus our coming King, High Priest, and Friend with our lives in the next life that He alone is the access to and rejoice with great joy and anticipation.

So to answer the question "Where am I going?" I would say that there is certainty that we can know where we should be going in God's plan for our lives both in this world and the next. We are responsible and accountable to Him as to what we do with His offer of salvation in the New Covenant, and how we handle ourselves in this life as being obedient to His Call on our lives and as a preparation for our eternal state in which we will only know joy when we are "in Him".

Questions on Chapter 9

1. What is the difference between a convert and a disciple?

2. Why does the realization of Covenant and its terms give us such a good framework in which to build our lives?

3. Why does modern Society and our world today clash so radically with the Covenanting Christian?

4. Paul contrasted "works of the flesh" with "fruit of the Spirit"—why did he use crucifixion as a process of moving from one to the other?

5. What links do you perceive between being a Temple of the Holy Spirit and bringing forth the "fruit of the Spirit"?

6. Reference was made to God's Action Plan for our lives. What does this consist of, and what is it referred to as by some?

7. By what means can we find out what this Action Plan is for each one of us?

8. Why can we be confident that this action Plan can be depended on no matter how impossible the circumstances may appear?

9. Why does the Resurrection of Jesus take on such significance when we consider our future life that He promised?

10. What is the link between the promised heavenly place that Jesus spoke of preparing for us, and our living in this life in the New Covenant?

10

CONCLUSION

I suppose to head a final Chapter of this book "Conclusion" begs the question, is there a conclusion to this subject? Of course the answer is that there will be no conclusion this side of Eternity. Herein is the core of the message of this book.

The next thing that has become apparent to me in writing this book is that as I write, more and more comes to mind that should be included, and I think you will have gathered that especially in the last Chapter. So I suppose such an outcome is really begging me to write more, but that will have to be a second or more books in covering more thoroughly the application of Covenant to various Doctrines and Practices that have been in the Church through the ages.

In concluding this book I would hope that I have been able to share with the reader the basics of the Christian Faith in a way that is generally little known but is the bedrock of our salvation and though lost to many, is a source of strength and comfort to those who have grasped the truth of Covenant and stabilized their lives no matter what came their way either in a natural or spiritual assault, and no matter the time frame in which they lived. The simple reason for these things is that we are dealing with eternal issues in this Covenant, and that means it is timeless and without limit in its scope.

If by writing this book, it causes those who read it to be greater in understanding of their salvation and the framework in which it is set, if it causes them to "reach into God" and dare to be the people He desires and intends they should be, if it causes them to communicate the Gospel of Jesus Christ in its fullness and glory to others in their generation, then it will have reached its goal that Christ may be glorified through all our lives, to His praise and glory. In finally, finally, concluding this book, I ask the reader this—to do something with the knowledge he or she has gained; do not let it fall to the ground, but by the Holy Spirit's anointing break through to new grounds of application, and fulfil your Calling—just be blessed from above and learn to receive what He has for you. Hope to see you in His nearer Presence!

Bibliography of works researched in preparation of this book

1. *Miracle of the Scarlet Thread*—Richard Booker—Destiny Image

2. *The Blood Covenant*—H. Clay Trumbull—Impact Christian Books

3. *Flesh & Blood: A History of the Cannibal Complex*—Reay Tannahill—Book Club Associates

4. *The Power of the Blood of Jesus*—Andrew Murray—Whitaker House

5. *Prophet of the Covenant*—Robert Watson—Collins

6. *The Blood Covenant*—E. W. Kenyon—Kenyon's Gospel Publishing Society

7. *New Covenant Realities*—Kevin J Conner—KJC Publications

8. Spiritual Warfare—Derek Prince—Whitaker House

9. War on the Saints—Jessie Penn-Lewis with Evan Roberts—Thomas Lowe Publishers with Diasozo Trust

10. Holy Bible—several versions researched

Identification of numbered references

1. *Miracle of the Scarlet Thread*—Richard Booker—p27.

2. *The Blood Covenant*—H. Clay Trumbull—p. 5.

3. Ibid—p. 10.

4. *Flesh and Blood: A History of the Cannibal Compex*—Reay Tanna-
    hill

5. *The Blood Covenant*—H. Clay Trumbull—p. 62.

6. *Prophet of the Covenant*—Robert Watson—p. 3.

978-0-595-38866-0
0-595-38866-3

Printed in the United States
101102LV00005BA/244/A